THE WAY OF
CALM

This edition first published in Great Britain in 2018 by
Eddison Books Limited
St Chad's House, 148 King's Cross Road
London WC1X 9DH
www.eddisonbooks.com

British Library Cataloguing-in-Publication data available on request.

ISBN 978-1-85906-069-8

10 9 8 7 6 5 4 3 2 1

Typeset in Minion Pro and TT Lakes using InDesign on Apple Macintosh
Printed in Europe

MIKE ANNESLEY
AND STEVE NOBEL

THE WAY OF
CALM

120 SIMPLE CHANGES TO HELP YOU FIND PEACE
IN A STRESSFUL WORLD

eddison
BOOKS LIMITED

CONTENTS

FOREWORD
BY STEVE NOBEL

I am no stranger to stress and anxiety. I was born into a family where there seemed more anxiety than peace and calm. Despite this, I managed to escape by diving into sports. I quite enjoyed school, even though there was a certain amount of pressure with exams. My real stress began when I entered the world of work. My father did not really agree with the idea of my following an academic path after my A levels, and told me to get a proper job. With this in mind, I used my head rather than my heart to choose a career, and this meant I faced some challenging consequences for many years. My head told me to get a secure job, and so I went to work in the financial sector in the City of London. The work was both highly dull and at times stressful. An early marriage added to the mix, and by the age of 25 I was the father of two young children. Later came divorce, career change and many other major upheavals in my life. In my early fifties, I went through a major life transition, which was very difficult: it took me nearly five years to navigate through it. So, I hope all this makes it clear that whatever I say about stress and calm comes from personal experience.

It's through experience that I know too much stress can utterly destroy our sense of calm; also, that stress is not only generated externally. We often unwittingly train our minds into fixating on problems of the past or upon desires, wishes or fantasies that hover in some distant and potentially unobtainable future. We often train our minds to be constantly on the go, like an engine that has no off switch.

This book addresses the ways we generate stress internally. It also looks at how we can improve the quality and direction of our thinking, thereby placing ourselves on an alternative path. This will have a positive effect on our emotional lives and on the way we act and move through the world. All this alone changes everything; but I believe there is more. Once stress has been reduced to a manageable level, then we can embrace the presence of something new. That presence could be defined as a state of mind or of being. I do not agree with the *Oxford Dictionary*'s definition of calm as merely the "absence" of something. I understand it to be not only the absence of something stressful or anxiety-creating but also the presence of something profoundly enriching.

I am now on my fourth career, which involves writing, coaching and healing. Through working with many people over the years in workshops and one-to-one coaching sessions, I understand the uniqueness of human beings. Because of this, I have little doubt that we all experience stress and also calm in different ways. It is true that calm *in part* involves the absence of something, but I also feel it includes the presence of an expansive and uplifting energy. Mental and emotional qualities such as peace, stillness, clarity, presence, joy and appreciation can all be important elements of calm.

One of the core assumptions of this book is that calm is always possible, no matter what the circumstances are. Life is difficult, unpredictable and, at times, volatile. Yet, if we prepare for challenge, rather than just meeting it head-on as it occurs, then we have a whole different experience of the encounter. This book can be of help during times of high stress, but it is also intended to be useful when the rug has not yet been pulled from under your feet. Working with the suggestions and exercises will help you prepare mentally and emotionally for the inevitable times when life does not go according to plan, as well as encourage you to think and act in ways that will lead you to the deep core of peace that lies within us all.

INTRODUCTION
STRESS AND CALM

Many people talk about the possibility of being calm, peaceful, at ease, without really believing they can ever achieve such a desirable state of mind. Life itself seems to have inbuilt characteristics that make this impossible. If it isn't one thing troubling us, making us anxious or stressed, it's another. Unease comes to be seen as a permanent aspect of our inner landscape – part of ourselves.

The basic principle behind this book is that the perception of stress as unavoidable is untrue: unease is *not* part of ourselves, it is a response we make and, like all responses, it falls within our powers of control. We can *choose* the way of calm.

At times, our circumstances may be more than usually challenging. We may be under pressure from juggling more than one role, or there may have been some shock that has stopped us in our tracks – perhaps redundancy, or a flood in the home, or the loss of someone dear. Then again, we might feel continually troubled because we are in an unrewarding relationship or job, cannot pay our bills or have reasons buried deep in our past that foster a low opinion of our own worth. For either of these two kinds of difficulties – the acute and the chronic – there are strategies we can bring to bear to regain our inner peace.

This book concentrates on two areas of experience where we can effectively make changes for the better – our thoughts and our actions. A third area, our emotions, is less controllable. Attempting to suppress an emotion would be self-defeating in any case, causing a build-up of confusion and anxiety. A more productive approach is always to acknowledge the emotions you feel and then make choices independently of them. This is a technique that can be learned. To reaffirm a key sentence above, we can *choose* the way of calm.

This choice will involve some kind of change, in either our circumstances or the way we respond to them, or both. Either type of change might fall anywhere on the spectrum, from easy to challenging. Change, whether self-initiated or imposed on us externally, can be seen as inherently stressful or as a journey of adventure: again we have a choice. Much will depend upon our attitude to risk and to the unknown future; and upon whether we can draw on our own strengths and on support, both practical and emotional, from other people.

Unease is often fuelled by dissatisfaction. An invaluable exercise is to consider whether any dissatisfaction we have with any dimension of our lives might be illusory. Dissatisfaction implies a view of how things ought to be, and we would do well to ask ourselves whether that view is founded on false assumptions. Often, if we know how to look, we can find happiness near at hand, in our existing situation, rather than in some distant place on which we set our sights. Related to this is the question of gratitude – what we take for granted, what we would truly appreciate if we stopped churning over our hopes and fears and started to really focus on what we have now.

Our values, and the degree by which we try to live by them, also play a major part in our journey towards peace. Two important elements here are our authenticity and our compassion – the way we relate to ourselves and the way we relate to others.

Meditation and other mind–body–spirit practices can be enormously helpful on the way of peace, and this book recommends that you build an appropriate discipline into your life. But the main emphasis in these pages is on the progress you can make by thinking about and acting on – in the light of universal truths – the triggers of unease and how you can learn to circumvent them.

How to be strong
AGAINST
STRESS

We may be aware of stress as part of our experience without knowing how deep is the damage it's causing us. Stress is insidious – even when we tell people how stressed we are, we may not take this enemy seriously enough. It's worth summoning all our resources to ensure that we reduce the stress in our lives.

But what if our circumstances are inherently stressful? What if we are juggling responsibilities at home and at work, or struggling financially and see no sure way

"The greatest weapon against stress is our ability to choose one thought over another."

WILLIAM JAMES (1842–1910)

"Tension is who you think you should be. Relaxation is who you are."

CHINESE PROVERB

to make ends meet? All of us face pressures, which sometimes push us in different directions at once. The real question is: do those pressures result in *internal* stress, harming our minds and bodies? They need not, so try asking yourself these three questions. Are there changes I should make to the way I lead my life? Can I improve my responses to difficult situations, to reduce levels of anxiety? Are there positive disciplines I can adopt to make myself more resilient?

The anatomy of
STRESS

**Stress is a response to a particular set of circumstances –
a situation we are struggling to deal with. That response is
often a mixture of physical, mental, emotional and behavioural
manifestations. A common experience, and one that most
obviously undermines our chances of contentment, is a
general feeling of anxiety, combined with an inability to relax.**

Stress may be defined as the body's reaction to a perceived pressure or
challenge, usually one of considerable duration – though even a single
event, such as an item of bad news, may cause long-term harm. The physical
effects may include sleeplessness, headaches, nausea, sweating, palpitations
or muscle tension. It's also understood that existing medical problems, such
as high blood pressure, may be worsened by stress.

Even if we manage to steer clear of actual illness, the emotional and
psychological effects of stress are no less damaging, because they too have
an impact on our levels of life satisfaction. We may feel disappointed in our
own inability to cope well under pressure, in which case the lowering of
self-esteem undermines our effectiveness still further, resulting in a vicious
spiral. We may become tearful or lonely, or sink into dark moods, incapable
of any positive thinking or action. On the mental level, we may find it
difficult to concentrate, and our memory may suffer.

The effects of stress on our behaviour may also be harmful. For example,
we may become unpunctual, or more generally unreliable – as if our
increased self-concern came at the expense of our responsible interest in the
convenience or welfare of others. The most harmful behavioural symptom,
without doubt, is the retreat into bad habits of eating and drinking and, all
too often, smoking or drug-taking. Addiction can set in quickly and, once
established, is hard to reverse.

The underlying picture

We all know people who seem to take stress in their stride – some, indeed,
seem to thrive on it, especially in the workplace. Other people, though,
seem to go to pieces when faced by even a minor setback, such as a home
appliance breaking down or a parcel going astray. The truth is, we all react
to stress differently.

STRESS SYMPTOM
checklist

Any of the symptoms listed here may indicate that you are feeling the effects of stress. The first step in working towards a cure is to gain self-knowledge. If you can tick off any of these effects as applying to you, consider how often and how strongly you experience them.

 THE PSYCHOLOGICAL REALM

- Inability to concentrate
- Indecisiveness
- Memory lapses
- Vagueness
- Tendency to be easily distracted
- Reduced creativity
- Negative thinking
- Anxiety and depression

THE EMOTIONAL REALM

- Tearfulness
- Irritability and anger
- Mood swings
- Sensitivity to criticism
- Defensiveness
- Feeling out of control
- Reduced motivation
- Frustration
- Reduced confidence
- Reduced self-esteem

THE PHYSICAL REALM

- Muscle tension
- Teeth grinding
- Susceptibility to colds or infections
- Skin irritations or rashes
- Digestive problems
- Weight loss or gain
- Ulcers
- Dizziness
- Palpitations
- Panic attacks
- Nausea
- Fatigue
- Loss of sexual desire
- High blood pressure
- Hypertension

THE BEHAVIOURAL REALM

- Inability to relax
- Neglect of leisure activities
- Resorting to alcohol, smoking, caffeine or drugs
- Overwork
- Absenteeism
- Neglect of fitness and personal appearance
- Social withdrawal
- Relationship issues
- Sleeplessness
- Recklessness
- Lying and making excuses

Three factors may predispose us towards high stress levels:

➲ The nature of the stress trigger and how persistently it operates on us.
➲ Our personality, which to a large degree may be genetically determined.
➲ The effectiveness of coping mechanisms that we habitually apply.

When the symptoms provoked by a particular trigger seem disproportionate, this may point to underlying issues in our lives. For example, if you have low self-esteem, leading to a deep-seated need for approval, a failure to get your boss to upgrade your job title (say, by adding the word "senior") may take on exaggerated dimensions, causing sleepless nights and other problems.

Starting a
STRESS JOURNAL

Monitoring your stress over time in a daily log can be helpful. Write up an entry each time you feel stressed, with notes under the following headings:

➲ TIME AND DATE

➲ TRIGGER

➲ BACKGROUND SITUATION

➲ HOW I REACTED: EMOTIONS AND SYMPTOMS

➲ INTENSITY OF STRESS (0 = very low, 10 = very high)

➲ HOW I RESPONDED: WORDS AND ACTIONS

➲ RESOLUTION

Look out for patterns you can learn from. Consider the triggers and what they have in common. What kinds of response to stress tend to bring the best resolution? As well as logging your stresses, write down anything at all you find calming – perhaps a comment someone makes or something in your reading. There's no need to make your journal neat and systematic. Think of it as the repository of your highly original, probably untidy, inner life.

THE STRESS TEST

To help reduce the stress in your life, you first need to recognize its causes. It might be easy enough to identify an emotive trigger, such as moving house or getting divorced, or a set of ongoing pressures on your time, but it often takes considerable self-knowledge to pinpoint the reasons for *chronic* stress. Try to build up a picture of your temperament and your circumstances based on which of these statements seem to match your situation (in brackets are some suggestions for possible approaches):

"Stress is built into my personality – I tend to overthink situations and worry needlessly about a whole lot of things at once."
(This suggests the need for inner work. It will help if you can learn to put small problems into perspective.)

"Pressures are piling up on me all the time, from all directions. The to-do list seems to get longer all the time."
(Perhaps you find it hard to say "no"? Try laying down some red lines, and take a more rigorous approach to time management.)

"I have so much to do, and that means I can't do any of it well enough. I don't like being forced to give less than my best."
(Perfectionism is often problematic. It might be better to compromise on your standards, aiming for "adequate" in some areas rather than "perfect".)

"Nobody understands how difficult things are for me. I wish people would just cut me some more slack."
(Until you accept some responsibility for at least contributing to your own problems, your levels of stress will always remain out of your control.)

How to deal with STRESS

One of the most reassuring things we can learn about stress is that we all have the power to have less of it. That is because our reaction to stress is always a matter of personal choice. By taking responsibility for our own thoughts, emotions and behaviour in response to stress, we can start to loosen its hold.

Once you have recognized the causes of your stress, there's a range of approaches you can take to try to banish it from your life. Consider the situations that are problematic for you and decide whether you could make changes in them. Some helpful areas for adjustment might include:

➔ **HOW YOU SPEND YOUR TIME** Time management, based on good preparation and organization, the ability to focus without being distracted, and clarity about your goals and the steps needed to achieve them, is a key aspect of being effective at home and at work. The big question of how you achieve a satisfactory life–work balance is relevant here, too. Sometimes a radical decision will resolve a problem – for example, leaving a job that requires four hours of commuting every day.

➔ **HOW YOU JUDGE YOUR PRIORITIES** A great deal of worry and wasted effort can result if you have no clear idea of what really matters to you or what you can spend less time on without letting yourself or others down. Clarify your priorities and be prepared to adjust them as the need arises.

➔ **HOW YOU USE SUPPORT FROM OTHERS** Emotional support is vital, but it's also good to identify sources of practical help. Clarify your needs and work out who can be useful – different people will probably be appropriate for different kinds of support. Many find it difficult to delegate, but this is a vital life skill.

You need to examine how you respond to stress, too. Perhaps your current coping strategies are inadequate, requiring you to put more long-term solutions in place, including lifestyle changes and new ways of using your downtime. The road map to stress reduction on the opposite page is intended as a basic introduction to this large and complex subject. You won't win the war against stress by concentrating on a single front. A holistic approach, amounting to a whole new set of attitudes and practices – a makeover, if you like – is likely to be more successful. That said, quick-fix techniques can help you get through stressful situations more comfortably (see pages 19–20).

A STRESS-REDUCTION
road map

Reducing stress usually requires work on two fronts: the circumstances of the situation from which the stress emerges; and your response to the triggers, which is largely within your own control once you have learned the necessary techniques.

Both sides of the equation are summarized below, with possible approaches listed. A lifestyle plan then follows on page 18, designed to help you to live in peace with yourself and with your responsibilities and pressures.

CHANGING YOUR SITUATION

- Saying "no" more often
- Doing less
- Managing your priorities better
- Being more productive
- Getting more help
- Doing something else

CHANGING YOUR RESPONSE

- Thinking more positively
- Judging yourself more kindly
- Valuing yourself more
- Acting more confidently
- Communicating better
- Behaving with more detachment

Lifestyle plan:
LIVING MORE ...

⊙ **HEALTHILY** A healthy diet and plenty of exercise, without any addictions or indulgences, build our resilience.

⊙ **AUTHENTICALLY** Being more true to yourself or your values removes a potential source of inner stress.

⊙ **MINDFULLY** Mindfulness, based on appreciating the present moment rather than worrying about the future or regretting the past, is one of many mind–body–spirit disciplines that can help you to reduce stress.

⊙ **GRATEFULLY** An appreciation of what we have, and the contribution made by others, is an effective antidote to stress.

⊙ **NATURALLY** Spending time within nature, whether camping or enjoying long walks in the countryside or in city parks, is a time-honoured corrective against life's everyday pressures.

⊙ **SIMPLY** Simplifying your life, with less attachment to material possessions and the trappings of a "successful" lifestyle, can bring greater contentment.

⊙ **SPIRITUALLY** A belief in the spirit and a concern for our own spiritual welfare put worldly stresses into perspective and thereby diminish their importance.

"Whenever you are asked if you can do a job, tell 'em, 'Certainly I can!' Then get busy and find out how to do it."

THEODORE ROOSEVELT (1858–1919)

Stress reduction
QUICK FIXES

Quick and easy methods for keeping stress under control are usually based on simple breathing techniques or on the art of mental distraction – by taking your mind away from a situation, you can sometimes regain a more balanced perspective.

Stress is seldom experienced evenly. There will be peaks of high stress that rise from time to time above a general level of vague dissatisfaction or even quiet neutrality as you encounter particular triggers. Many time-honoured techniques for weathering these little storms of emotion involve taking deep breaths, since breathing more deeply increases the flow of oxygen to the brain, which in turn helps you to take control of your stress symptoms and relax your muscles. Below are five quick fixes to assist you in dealing with difficult situations, whether you take a pause in the middle of the situation itself or practise the exercise prior to a forthcoming event that is making you anxious – for example, an interview or test, or a worrying confrontation.

1 FOUR-BY-FOUR WALKING

This is a simple way to lower nervous tension. Walk around whatever space is available (in a circle, if necessary) to a rhythmic count: inhaling for four steps, then exhaling for the next four, inhaling again for four steps … and so on. Do this for at least three minutes. You could progress to a more advanced form, with six or even eight steps for each in-breath and out-breath.

2 SIMPLE PEACE AFFIRMATION

Sit comfortably and take a few slow, deep breaths. Continue this while repeating the words "I am" silently to yourself as you breathe in, and "at peace" as you breathe out. Do this three or four times. Then let your whole body go loose as you sit in the chair, releasing your tensions.

3 POCKET MINDFULNESS

Carry in your pocket an item with positive associations. Possibilities might include a photograph or an item of jewellery given by someone you love. When you feel stress levels building, spend a few minutes meditating on the item, focusing on the experience of perceiving it visually – and perhaps also by touch – within the present moment. Look at all aspects of the physical thing, then relish its personal associations. Draw upon its energy to give you strength, confidence and courage.

4 VIEW FROM AFAR

When we're stressed, our challenges can assume exaggerated proportions. It can be therapeutic to step back and look at the situation from afar. Close your eyes and imagine being beamed up to a satellite and using a high-powered telescope to zoom in on what is stressing you. Then zoom out and see this alongside the stresses others in the world are experiencing. When you open your eyes again, think of yourself as transformed in wisdom by your view from space.

5 FURTHER QUICKIES

Once you have tried one or two of these quick fixes, try devising your own quick fix, perhaps with an element of breath control, creative visualization or affirmation, or a combination of these ingredients. Make your exercise relate in some way to what you value in life. For example, if you are a keen chess player, you might carry a king or queen with you, as a source of regal power, or a knight, as a shamanic talisman to promote nimble thinking.

Two final tips:
- Take regular breaks from any extended activity. Even if you are just doing jobs in the home, get out every couple of hours.
- Try to keep your sense of humour. Spend time with a friend who makes you laugh.

The art of
ACCEPTANCE

The unexpected can throw us off-balance, stirring up emotions and distracting us from normal life. To accept unwelcome change, we need to be patient with ourselves while we learn to adjust to new realities. The same kind of approach is invaluable in ongoing situations that have become hard to accept – such as a never-diminishing in-tray.

When something disappoints us or thwarts our plans, or we're given bad news, it's often impossible to process the new situation quickly. And yet we're likely to regard the matter as urgent. If so, this tends to be because of emotions that make us react immediately, even when a quick response is unlikely to produce the best outcome.

Stepping back and positioning the setback within a suitable mental timeframe can be difficult, since emotions are always crying out to us to be noticed and acted upon. Silencing the cry of emotions – the art of detachment – is an invaluable life skill.

Philosophically it isn't difficult to grasp the basic principle for putting acceptance into practice: change what we can change, accept what we can't. The reality, however, is not so straightforward. There are a number of complicating factors, which are given here with optimum responses you might wish to adopt:

- ➥ Often it isn't clear which aspects of the situation are within our control and which are beyond our influence – *assess what you think you can influence and judge your likelihood of success.*
- ➥ At the emotional level we may find it difficult to accept uncomfortable truths – *identify the emotions you have and don't judge yourself for having them.*
- ➥ It can be easier to immerse ourselves in an uncomfortable situation than to walk away from it temporarily – *try to absorb yourself in something else for a while; then, when you come back to the problem, see if you have any new insights to apply.*

Accept or change?

The main complication here is that we tend to entertain possible solutions to any problem, even if none of them is likely to bear fruit. For example, if a partner leaves you for someone else, you might entertain the idea of winning them back, even though their mind seemed made up when they

THE SETBACK
questionnaire

When a "bad" situation arises – anywhere on the spectrum, from disappointing to devastating – ask yourself the following questions (given here with practical tips for answering them satisfactorily).

What is the positive side of the new situation?
(there will often be one if you can apply your imagination to the matter)

What is my emotional response?
(allow yourself to feel strong emotions, but bear in mind it can be helpful to try to identify them too)

What practical steps can I take to make things better?
(these might range from enlisting help from a friend to forming an action plan to mitigate the damage)

Do I need to explain the situation to anyone?
(you might need, for example, to pull out of some commitments, or ask for other people's understanding)

Can anyone else help me deal with the practicalities?
(good friends can be helpful in making concrete suggestions or doing errands for you)

Where can I find support to help me deal with my troubled emotions?
(it's unhealthy to try to deal with emotional crises on your own)

What could I do in the short term?
(possibilities might range from making a few explanatory phone calls to taking a break from the stress)

What plans would I like to make for the future, and when?
(before you make plans, it's often best to wait until all the new circumstances are clear)

told you about their feelings. There would be no harm in *trying* to win them over, certainly. If you have children, there are family considerations, and it would be irresponsible not to talk through all the alternatives. A completely different situation would be the difficulty you might have in accepting the new partnership – for example, after the couple had moved in together or got married. The matter then becomes one of emotions rather than practicalities. And negative emotions, such as jealousy or envy, need to be addressed mindfully (see page 83) if you seek to restore your tranquillity.

Clearly, you need to separate emotional and practical responses. A practical response to an uncomfortable situation will always carry a tinge of emotion, such as regret, jealousy or frustration, but in choosing how to act you must try to assess the practical element in purely practical terms. If you want to win them back, how feasible is this? Don't let your emotions colour the answer.

THE ACCEPTANCE CURVE

This graph shows the changes you might need to go through to accept a major unsought change in your life.

AFFIRMATION
I'm acknowledging the new reality

COMMITTING TO THE FUTURE

COMMITMENT
I'm undertaking to adjust accordingly

ACCEPTANCE
I'm learning to live with the new situation

CONSIDERATION
I'm looking at all aspects of the new situation

REACHING ACCEPTANCE

COMPREHENSION
I'm seeing how the change will affect me

AWARENESS
I'm learning the nature of the change

PROCESSING THE FACTS

INFORMATION
I'm discovering change is happening

The art of
POSITIVE CHANGE

In stressful circumstances we often feel like having a *complete* change. Although this is often merely daydreaming, the truth is that we *can* bring about a transformative change if we know exactly what our goals are and take considered and realistic steps towards achieving them.

As we have seen, there are three areas of change we need to consider when trying to combat stress: (1) The situation; (2) Our response to the situation; (3) Our attitudes and lifestyle in general.

Changing the situation (1) will involve taking practical steps, but first you need to take a detached look at your whole predicament. When emotions come into play, you will need to recognize them and make allowances for them – do your strong feelings colour and even distort your perceived picture? In answering this question, you may see the need for making changes in your responses (2), affecting the way you process your experiences inwardly. Then, in turn, you might broaden this insight to accept that you need to change your attitudes (3) – being less perfectionist or less judgmental, for example. "Lifestyle" is mentioned because transformative change of this kind is more likely to be successful if you start living with greater self-awareness and take more responsibility for your fulfilment. This will involve cutting out bad habits and adopting good ones.

The only way to make positive change happen in your life is by making choices. In fact, we make more choices than we imagine, misleadingly attributing elements of our lives that are totally within our control to one of these two factors:

1 NORMS For example, shaking a friend's hand instead of hugging them, taking a holiday every year or trying for another child.

2 HABITS For example, battling through the rush hour in your daily commute or watching TV with your partner in the evenings.

When thinking about what to change, it's helpful to question the norms, since they might be more flexible than you assume. Although some people may perform a task one particular way, you might find that nobody minds if you do it differently. Even if they did, perhaps you should assert your right to choose. As for habits, you must refuse to accept their authority over you, since a habit is simply a choice made repeatedly – it's not automatic, though it may seem so.

GUIDELINES FOR CHANGE

Here are some practical tips for anyone committed to making changes in their life in order to reduce stress levels.

● THINK SMALL AT FIRST

Do you need to make one large, radical change, or would it be better to make a number of smaller changes to aspects of a situation? To answer this, try considering the small changes first, as often they will suffice. You may end up with a long list to work through, but this may be easier than doing something more drastic. If not, move on to think seriously about a more radical approach. Weigh the two options – one large change versus many small ones – carefully, taking your time.

● PRACTISE CHANGE

This may seem strange, but if you can break a few small habits while you are deciding what changes to make, it can be useful in preparing yourself for the required flexibility. Every expedition outside your comfort zone will help you to build a change-ready mindset.

● USE A TIME CUE

When deciding on a change, schedule a particular moment when you will put it into action. It may be a date on the calendar (it sometimes helps to fix upon a time, as well) or it may be the next occasion that something happens – for example, next time you are sharing a meal with your partner. Choose mornings in preference to afternoons – you will have the rest of the day in which to celebrate your decisiveness.

● PICTURE THE OUTCOME

Imagining how things will be after the change
is an effective motivator. Build up a vivid image of
the new situation, with significant details to symbolize
the improvement. Mentally rehearse the image
to let it sink in. Summon it and draw upon
its positive energy when
motivation flags.

● PREPARE YOUR SUPPORT

It's helpful not only to have a support network in
place, but also to brief its members in advance
about what you are planning. Gauge the help each
individual can give, remembering that practical and
emotional help may come from different people.

● MAKE RATHER THAN BREAK

When you put an end to a habit, think of this
in positive rather than negative terms. It was
the habit itself that was negative. Once you
have adopted a new positive habit, you may well
be able to leverage it into a larger transformation
in your behaviour.

● PROGRESS IN STAGES

Taking one small step, than another, will move you more
reliably towards the larger goal. Attempting to make
changes on too many fronts simultaneously might
only add to the stress. Write up each significant step
forwards in your journal, acknowledging achievement.

Lowering your
STRESS LEVELS

3 AFFIRMATIONS

➡ "I'm reducing my stress, by taking ownership of my situation. I'm the only one in charge here."

➡ "I'm stepping back from my emotions and assessing their causes. I'm learning from self-scrutiny."

➡ "I'm following my own path, detaching myself from any unrealistic expectations from others. I feel no guilt over finding my own solutions."

7 THOUGHT POINTS

➡ Put stress in perspective

Many of our stresses are over issues that are intrinsically unimportant, in any true scale of values. Workplace stresses in particular come into this category. It can help to remind yourself of what you really value in life – especially the sources of love and your own sense of personal authenticity. Measured on such a scale, your issues may suddenly appear more trivial – which does not mean that you should give up trying to resolve them. When your stress is more radical, stemming from trauma or loss, the main thing is to give yourself permission to be upset, and to have faith in love and spirit to see you through.

➡ Refuse to be diminished

Stressful situations, especially those related to being overstretched or overcommitted, are often claustrophobic. You may feel you are being pressed from all sides. It's important in such circumstances not to feel that you are diminished – reduced to being an agent of someone else's will, or forced to narrow your horizons to allow time and energy for particular tasks or responsibilities. You remain, always, your essential self, no matter what circumstances are limiting the full expression of that self. Don't allow yourself to be defined by the stress you are under.

➲ Break it down

Having a huge number of items on your to-do list, or being immersed in a large undertaking that is proving overpowering, can sometimes engender a pervasive sense of failure. Break down the pressures that are impinging on you – for example, divide large projects into smaller steps or bits. Set boundaries around your time and in-tray. Be sure to celebrate any measure of success – either rising to one of many small challenges, or achieving a good outcome in one aspect of a larger one.

➲ Switch focus

A stressful problem can pull you in. You might dwell on it even when you are elsewhere, supposedly doing something else. You may feel your emotional life now points perpetually towards that unresolved issue. Don't let this happen. As soon as you feel your thoughts drifting back to stress triggers, switch your focus to a completely different part of your life. Clear space for other emotions, including joy. Immerse yourself in the good when you can do nothing about the bad.

➲ Smile at absurdity

Stressful situations often have an absurd dimension, which may prove to be humorous. A tyrannical boss or even a demanding partner or relative may one day strike you as funny. You may find yourself going to ridiculous lengths to deal with the pressures placed on you. Step outside your situation from time to time and see it as a stranger would – it might then appear hilarious. Tell someone the story of your day: sharing an experience often helps you to see the funny side, and this can make it retrospectively less painful.

➲ Let storms rage

Sometimes we might find ourselves in environments where all is chaos – people panicking, arguments breaking out, everything going wrong. So long as you are giving your best, there's no need to be drawn into the whirlpool of others' emotions. By all means try to soothe hurt feelings or defuse any anger, but, if this fails, sometimes the best policy is to wait until the storm subsides, while staying as detached as possible. When the emotional temperature rises, it often makes sense to reschedule a conversation, change the subject or just make an excuse and find a more peaceful setting for your activities.

➲ Look from all angles

Many stresses are shared. Observe how others deal with the stresses that impact on you. If you are in conflict with another person, seeing things from their perspective can help you find a resolution. Or, if you both face the same pressures, you might learn from the other person's coping strategies. Looking at any situation from the viewpoint of others involved can be rewarding. It may make you understand why you cannot take a shortcut through the complexities.

ACTION PLAN

Taking charge of
YOUR STRESS

10 ACTION POINTS

➔ Redesign the pattern

In many stressful situations there is a pattern. This could be a method of operating, a hierarchy or a balance of compensations. To take a domestic example, one partner in a couple might be responsible for routine household matters while the other has sole responsibility for problem-solving. Identify the patterns in your situation and which elements you want to change. Then assess any factors that might make such an adjustment difficult. Consider how to deal with these factors and put your optimum changes into effect.

➔ Choose what to lose

Most stressful situations have an element you would ideally like to see disappear. Your first attempt to identify this may not be realistic. For example, if you are a carer, there's no point in wishing your charge were younger and less dependent. But there may be something that could be removed from the situation that would help – perhaps a daily routine or an unrealistic expectation. Decide what to lose and how to go about it.

➔ Define what your role involves

We are often stressed by the pressure to do more in a role (whether a work role, a family role or otherwise) than we see as appropriate for ourselves. Define what the role means for you, then compare that with what seems to be expected. Consider what steps you need to take to narrow the gap between the two points, or somehow deflect the pressure.

➔ Take two to four breaks daily

In the middle of a stressful situation, there are several reasons why you might opt not to take a break. You might feel there's no time, or you might worry about what others may think, or you might have difficulty imagining yourself relaxing properly. However, take those breaks anyway. It's unhealthy not to have some respite for a protracted period of stress.

➲ Measure your progress

There are two ways to calibrate progress under stress. The first is to check how well you are doing in your tasks; the second is to measure how successful you are in feeling more peaceful or relaxed. Attend to the second of these priorities, even if it seems to involve downgrading the first.

➲ Weave rewards into your life

In any stressful situation there will be occasional cause for congratulation – if only you can suspend your negative thinking for a moment. Mark such moments and give yourself a reward to celebrate them. It could be something small-scale, such as allowing yourself to relax with a favourite music track. Celebrate with your partner or a friend if you feel the achievement might warrant this.

➲ Remember to give

The narrowing of horizons caused by stress can make us more self-absorbed, and therefore more selfish, than we would be otherwise. Make sure that you continue to give as freely as you can – try to be no less generous with your time, attention or compassion. Make magnanimous gestures when you can. Not least among the benefits of this is showing your stressors that they are not defeating you.

➲ Ask quality questions

In difficult situations, you may feel your voice is not contributing to a solution but only making your stress felt by others. It's worth seeing what happens if you ask constructive questions, such as "What would really make a difference here?" A well-judged question can set in motion changes that work in everyone's favour.

➲ Keep friendships alive

A stressful situation may act as a time thief, stealing hours that would otherwise be devoted to social life. Moreover, stress can make us less likely to seek company – we may even see ourselves as boring, preferring to brood at home. However, to neglect a friendship is to turn your back on potential support, as well as distraction. In any case, friendships are too valuable to sacrifice, however severe your stress. Make an effort to see friends, even if your encounter has to be shorter than usual. Try to avoid cancelling social commitments. Bear in mind that friends can offer unusual perspectives you may not have considered.

➲ Motivate an ally

Friends need no motivation to help you, other than the value of friendship itself, but they do need to know the facts, as well as the depth and urgency of the need they will be serving. It helps if you make it clear just how much their support means to you. Be as specific as possible in describing the consequences of their involvement. The same applies also to well-intentioned people who are not friends – but may become so.

How to find
CALM IN YOUR LIFE

Even those who would not describe themselves as stressed are, at times, likely to feel there are aspects of their lives they would like to change – factors that militate against their well-being. Lack of self-esteem and confidence are the twin pillars of unease for many: they go hand in hand like mischievous twins. These issues, even when not causing unhappiness, have the power to impede the realization of your full potential. This chapter offers a range of down-to-earth ways to address them.

CHAPTER 2

"Praise and blame, gain and loss, pleasure and sorrow come and go like the wind. To be happy, rest like a great tree in the midst of them all."

ACHAAN CHAA (d.1922)

On the more practical level, there is the question of time, which instead of being a neutral medium for living becomes an enemy of success and therefore fulfilment. Time-management skills are a vital key to a happier life. Allied to this is the benefit of living by well-defined personal priorities. Not only does this help us deal effectively with time pressures, but it also gives us a clearer sense of who we are and might become.

Befriending
TIME

All too readily time can seem like a force pitched against us, rather than the neutral medium of our life. There are occasions when we need to exert mastery over time, but in doing so we may, paradoxically, become time's slave. This can be avoided by taking a more flexible approach, whenever appropriate.

We tend to see time as a luxury: the sense of having plenty of time to do a chore, or to relax before our holiday ends, generates a good feeling. Conversely, not having enough time chips away at our peace of mind. Both attitudes commoditize time. When working to a deadline, we inevitably think like this, imagining the ongoing depletion of a finite resource. But when we become preoccupied with time's limits, we take our minds off the real point, which is the *quality* of whatever we are doing, whether performing a task or enjoying a break. We are robbed of focus and, if the experience is potentially enjoyable, of pleasure.

Flow and distraction
The opposite of time obsession is the flow state, or "being in the zone", when we become so absorbed in an activity that we lose awareness of time passing. Among the ingredients that encourage flow are curiosity and inspiration. Another is passion, since this involves giving something 100 per cent of your attention. Distraction is more likely when you are unenthusiastic. That's why an unwelcome chore can seem to take so long: even when there's a deadline, it can be hard to focus.

We find flow whenever we are fully focused on activity in the moment, and so it's worth cultivating a realm where this experience is readily available. It could be a leisure pursuit, such as gardening, model making, drawing, writing short stories, rock climbing, swimming or playing chess. Or it could be volunteering – for example, in social work of some kind. If work is your source of flow, you are

> "But what minutes! Count them by sensation, and not by calendars, and each moment is a day."
>
> BENJAMIN DISRAELI (1804–1881)

fortunate. The working day will seem briefer, you will less often feel flat, undervalued or exploited, and you are being paid for what you love.

Even in the most boring of jobs, there's always a source of flow to be found. There may be one task at which you particularly excel and that you can fully inhabit. Having a conscious intention to do the best work you possibly can will often take you part of the way to this optimum situation. And finding little points of humour can help you to find flow in challenging activities.

Time as a vehicle

It's healthy to think of time as the vehicle of fulfilment – just as the body is the vehicle of the soul. Time is not a resource, like paper or printer ink. Try to think of it as the free-flowing river in which we swim rather than a series of locks to be negotiated. Clock time has its place, especially in family life and work, but there's also much to be said for tuning yourself to your body's natural cycles – having a meal when you are hungry and going to bed when you are tired. This means recapturing something like a preindustrial mindset, before the clock regulated our working hours.

Hard and soft approaches

Sometimes, of course, you will need to manage your time carefully to master the tasks on your to-do list. Effectiveness, which means prioritizing urgent or important goals and doing them first, trumps efficiency, which can easily be focused in the wrong places. There's a whole repertoire of time-management techniques, including scheduling, progress reviewing, delegation and so on, which are largely common-sense but have been endlessly codified. These are the "hard" approaches to time management. On pages 36–7 are some "soft" approaches that offer a useful corrective, especially in the context of leading a calm, fulfilling life. To apply hard management methods to life's most precious dimension is a recipe for anxiety rather than true contentment.

GO SOFTLY WITH TIME

Never forget how precious time is – it cannot be replaced.
Good time management can help you towards the lifestyle
you seek, but be aware of the risk of applying rigid discipline in
areas where flexibility can lead to a happier result. Managing
your time can become a fetish that starts to manage you.
Below are five rewarding principles to follow.

1 BE WARY OF APPS

Time-management apps have their place, but it's easy to get fixated on
them or to imagine they can resolve any lifestyle tensions. In a relaxed life,
technology plays a subordinate role. Writing things down, in any case, has
the value of connecting you with a long tradition of self-expression on
paper – even if you are just making notes.

2 SET DIRECTIONS AS WELL AS GOALS

A goal is specific and fixed. In certain areas of life it's more appropriate to
set a direction, allowing yourself the flexibility to change course. Having
well-defined aims in every area of life is not desirable – on the whole, it's
better to live by values than by targets.

3 LET TIME UNFOLD

We seem to have lost the art of letting time patiently unfold. We apologize by text if we are going to be a few minutes late meeting a friend; if we are first to arrive in a café we text to say where we are sitting. This behaviour shows avoidable time anxiety. Don't treat meeting a friend like a military operation. See if you can allow each other more flexibility. Use waiting time as bonus time for thinking, watching, reading or meditating.

4 ENJOY UNPLANNED TIME

Try to have occasional days without structure, so that each activity is allowed its own natural time frame. It's fun to do this with a friend or partner, coming up with improvised plans on the move. Distractions become a source of pleasure rather than frustration. Being free to follow tangents can lead to exciting discoveries.

5 AVOID SELF-IMPOSED TIME TRAPS

When making a commitment to others, we often set unnecessarily tight deadlines for ourselves. Then, when we run late, we have the embarrassment of having to renegotiate. Better to say you prefer to be open-ended about the schedule. Sometimes it makes sense to specify an estimated time of completion once you are halfway through an activity.

BALANCING your needs

Some psychological needs are original to ourselves, while others are shared with everyone. Tensions between the various needs mean that not all can be met. Each person has a unique pattern of compromise that works best for them. Calm is achievable when you evaluate and live by your priorities.

Given the bewildering variety in human personality, it's perhaps surprising to be reminded how alike we all are in certain respects. According to a model of psychological needs proposed by the American psychologist Albert Maslow in 1943, we all need a sense of belonging to our social setting, alongside a desire for both love and esteem. At a higher level in the hierarchy of needs, we seek self-actualization – the fulfilment of our untapped inner potential.

At a more basic level is the following trio of needs proposed in self-determination theory, which was developed in the 1970s and 1980s:

1 AUTONOMY The sense of our exercising free choices and being responsible for our actions.

2 COMPETENCE The sense that we have control over our circumstances, including our environment.

3 RELATEDNESS The sense of being in meaningful relationships with other people.

On the opposite page is a more detailed model of needs. Despite differences, all three models agree on the importance we attach to relationships and participation in society. Being alone isn't an option, though we might choose to find company through friends and family rather than a romantic bond.

Finding equilibrium

As individuals, we remain distinct in the relative importance we attach to such needs. For example, a maverick might care little about the opinions of others, whereas someone insecure might rank them highly. Tensions between different values can be difficult to deal with. For example, if you pursue hard work you might find it difficult to give loving attention to your family.

Navigating between our needs is a lifelong challenge, magnified by the importance we all attach to relationships. Good communication skills can help you to steer a course that satisfies all parties, but an equal requirement is a willingness to compromise.

The circle of CONTENTMENT

The following system of psychological needs is based on the work of Artur Manfred Max Neef (b.1932), a Chilean economist. Each basic need is accompanied by a short list of factors that impinge upon it. Read around this circle and reflect on the relative importance of each dimension in your life now. Consider how the pie chart proportions would need to be adjusted to correspond to your ideal. What tensions do you perceive now and in your optimum model?

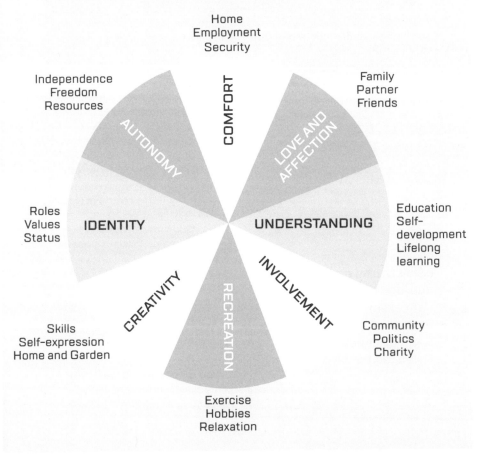

Home
Employment
Security

Independence
Freedom
Resources

Family
Partner
Friends

AUTONOMY

COMFORT

LOVE AND AFFECTION

Roles
Values
Status

IDENTITY

UNDERSTANDING

Education
Self-
development
Lifelong
learning

CREATIVITY

RECREATION

INVOLVEMENT

Skills
Self-expression
Home and Garden

Community
Politics
Charity

Exercise
Hobbies
Relaxation

SELF-VALUING

Any doubts we might have about our worth and ability tend to accumulate over time, creating a negative inner dialogue that eats into peace of mind. The key to correcting this delusion is to abolish our "negative self-talk" and replace it with a positive inner conversation, focusing on celebrating our successes.

Self-doubt, once it has taken root, can crystallize as a habitual thought pattern. We attribute negative adjectives to ourselves – unimaginative, unattractive, boring. Such critical inner voices tend to drown out even the positive messages our friends give us, so that we suspect them of well-intentioned insincerity when they praise us.

The best starting point for silencing the interior critic is to detach yourself from your thinking habits and observe them in a spirit of self-analysis. Once you have recognized low self-esteem, you can start to work on it. Look for the following indicators:

SOURCES OF SELF-DOUBT

Any of the following factors may result in low self-valuing, although equally common is the influence of upbringing, when a parent shows the tendency.

> Being bullied or abused
> Job loss or unemployment
> Poor exam results
> Stress
> Chronic illness
> Failed relationship

- When you feel neglected by a friend, acquaintance or family member, you blame yourself for upsetting them in some way.
- In situations where potentially you are judged by others – for example, in an interview, a social conversation with a stranger or while giving a speech – you feel a sense of personal inadequacy.
- You avoid putting yourself forward as a candidate for roles you would ideally like to fill, since you imagine you would be outshone by the competition.
- You live largely according to habit, avoiding new situations where you feel you would be likely to expose your own weaknesses.

Escape from negativity
Low self-valuing damages your relationship with yourself and with

REVERSING SELF-DOUBT

Self-doubt operates in a vicious cycle, represented below. It feeds off its own energy and grows bigger. However, once you have started to put in place a more positive view of your own value, this too can be self-perpetuating.

LOW SELF-ESTEEM ⟫ **Low expectation of success ⟫ Anxiety undermines success ⟫ Self-esteem lowered even more**

HIGH SELF-ESTEEM ⟫ **Increased motivation, effort and persistence ⟫ Success is achieved ⟫ Self-esteem raised even more**

others. It also makes it difficult to relax, as any empty time you have is likely to be filled with anxiety, which nags away at least at the subliminal level, if not explicitly.

To rebuild your self-image, try to put into effect a programme based around the following points:

- ➲ **BE COMPASSIONATE** towards yourself and forgiving of your mistakes – this is just as important as compassion to others.
- ➲ **ACCEPT AND CELEBRATE** your own individuality – the unique person you are.
- ➲ **FOLLOW YOUR PASSION** for its own sake, having faith that good things will follow.
- ➲ **IDENTIFY YOUR STRENGTHS** and utilize them as much as possible, relishing (whenever you have the opportunity) the sensation of doing things to a high standard of excellence.
- ➲ **CONTRIBUTE TO A GOOD CAUSE** – the knowledge that you have acted virtuously may unconsciously underpin your self-esteem.
- ➲ **SET CHALLENGES FOR YOURSELF** – overcoming the obstacles and achieving a goal is likely to make you feel stronger and more able.
- ➲ **AVOID PEOPLE WHO MAKE YOU FEEL SMALLER** – at least temporarily, although as your self-esteem builds you might decide to encounter them again as an interesting self-challenge.

CONFIDENCE tricks

Confidence stems largely from acceptance of who you are and what you can offer, based on evaluating both your previous experience and your potential. To some extent you can learn how to be confident even while working to repair flaws in your self-belief.

When we see people who come over as self-assured and capable, we think of them as exhibiting a personality trait. In fact, their level of faith in their own ability to perform roles and tasks is likely to rise and fall over time. They may show more confidence than they feel.

One key to acting confidently is accepting the inevitability of mistakes, especially when doing something new. When mistakes occur, you need to know how to get past them and move towards your goals. Planning and preparation are equally important. It's helpful to divide tasks into segments and plan as many as you can. Although, in meetings or difficult conversations, improvisational skill is called upon, mastery of the subject is the best way to ensure that your improvising is effective.

Being happy in your skin, clothes or personality is the essence of confidence. Bear in mind, though, that superficial changes – say, to your dress or hair – can only go so far. More important is to cultivate a relaxed, free-floating effectiveness. Always remember that you can at least equal your previous best and probably go beyond it.

Sneak thieves of confidence

Below are three common ways in which confidence can be undermined by unplanned events – with proposed guidelines for dealing with them.

APPEARANCE FLAWS

Noticing your cuffs are frayed or wishing you had cut your nails may niggle at your confidence. But if you are able to put such minor issues in perspective and then forget about them, there's no reason why you should not be able to carry on at full strength. Nobody else is going to worry.

MISTAKES

If you do an accidental backflip in a presentation or forget someone's name, don't allow space in your head for regret, which saps energy. Learn from your mistakes, but don't spend any time, while still in full flow, wondering how you could have made them.

SURPRISE INTERVENTIONS

However well prepared you are, it's good to be ready for surprises. Don't be so attached to the script that you are taken aback by the unexpected and unable to improvise. Go through some possible left-field scenarios before you set out.

TWO CONFIDENCE STYLES

There are two contrasting styles of confidence: the taut and the relaxed, with gradations in between. The relaxed style usually stems from a sense of well-being. If you can tap into this, your confidence will grow with experience.

TAUT CONFIDENCE	RELAXED CONFIDENCE
NARROW FOCUS Achieves goals by narrowing effort and excluding distraction	**OPEN FOCUS** Is prepared to consider other insights while pursuing a goal, finding distractions inspiring or enlightening
REJECTS CRITICISM Shuts out any voices expressing disagreement	**LEARNS FROM CRITICISM** Considers what others say, often gaining fresh insights from them
FIXED GOALS Decides on a plan and takes logical steps to attain the set aim	**FLEXIBLE GOALS** Is prepared to modify intention in the light of changing circumstances or new discoveries
Pitfalls: Arrogance ✖ Humourlessness ✖	Pitfalls: ✖ Indolence ✖ Indifference

Long-term PERSPECTIVES

Finding calm in your life is not just a matter of keeping stress at bay and learning self-valuing and confidence – the topics we have considered so far. A great deal of progress can be made by working on such issues, but for long-term calm you need to look at your whole relationship with yourself, with others and with life itself.

Two selves?

You may often imagine you are sharing your life with an interior self – the one who makes silent criticisms of yourself and others, and has a great deal of knowledge about both your strengths and weaknesses that's denied to other people, except perhaps your closest confidants. Much of the unease we are likely to deal with is accompanied by an increased sense of distance between the inner and the outer person. At one extreme this can lead to self-delusion and fantasy, where we retreat into our imaginations, reacting against a real world in which we feel alien. We might become aggressive, speaking whatever is on our minds. But even in relatively balanced people, the divided self can be a symptom of imbalance. The aim, when it comes to finding deep peace, is to ensure that our inbuilt division is perceived in other terms: as thinking and acting self, or private and public self, rather than real and false self. Ideally, there should be congruence between the two.

Public and private

There will always be thoughts we prefer to keep from others, and that is not necessarily a symptom of insincerity. Inner filters are necessary and beneficial. Imagine you have rushed to the aid of someone knocked off their bicycle by a speeding car. You will adopt a compassionate tone, saying nothing about how disturbing you find their injuries. When you are feeling strong emotion, you are not always going to tell people around you: if every emotion were accurately reported at the moment of experiencing it, society would become chaotic.

At the same time, communication is a fundamental strand in our well-being. By working on our communication skills, and in particular learning to speak slowly and thoughtfully on difficult subjects, we enrich our lives.

Here are three further points that are worth emphasizing:

1 BE MINDFUL OF MOMENTS We miss a great deal if we spend too much time regretting or analysing the past, or fretting anxiously about the future.

2 ACCEPT ENDINGS, EMBRACE BEGINNINGS It's fruitless to try to cling to a phase in life that is definitely over. Ageing rock stars who do this, unwilling to give up the touring life, may miss out on maturer pleasures. Let go of the past and look forwards.

3 BREATHE LOVE Even experiences of mishap and setback are refracted through love when we share them with our loved ones. Let love be your life's oxygen.

Road map for
CALM AND CONTENTMENT

To maximize your chances of living calmly and happily, it's rewarding to attend to the following five "relationships", listed here in terms of their individual components.

WITH YOURSELF
Self-esteem
Confidence
Authenticity
Compassion
Self-sacrifice

WITH OTHERS
Communication
Love
Respect
Empathy
Forgiveness

WITH THE PAST
Acceptance
Learning

WITH THE PRESENT
Attention
Gratitude

WITH THE FUTURE
Hope
Resolution

Finding
CALM HORIZONS

3 AFFIRMATIONS

➔ "I relish the unfolding of my life, with all its moments of stasis and change. I'm grateful for the gift of being here now."

➔ "I'm happy to be myself, on my endless journey of learning and growing. I release impossible longings and useless regrets."

➔ "My life is the unfolding canvas of creativity and love. Constantly I evolve in learning, committed to making the most of all challenges and opportunities."

7 THOUGHT POINTS

➔ Cultivate gratitude

Thankfulness is an outgoing energy and an effective antidote to unbridled ego. Its opposite is envy. If you find yourself envying someone's talent, status, possessions or opportunities, convert that by a mental somersault to gratitude on their behalf – and also be grateful for your own blessings, which are different but no less extraordinary. Living in a civilized democratic country with well-protected human rights is not least of the things you can be grateful for, if you are fortunate enough to enjoy this.

➔ Quietly reflect

Taking a few minutes to be reflective, sitting comfortably in a quiet place with the mobile phone switched off, can be an effective way to solve problems – not by mentally testing different hypothetical scenarios, or going through a list of pros and cons, but by creating space in your mind for insights to surface of their own volition. This is how intuition operates: a good thought dawns on you when you are still and at peace. Intuition is also the source of many creative concepts.

⊜ Question habits of thought

The opinions we have harboured can harden into unjustified presumptions or even prejudices if we are not careful. One of the most revealing "what if" speculations to entertain in your mind is "What if I am wrong?" Test your deeply held views in the light of new experiences and encounters – the stories you hear, the people you meet, the writings you read.

⊜ Curiouser and curiouser

Curiosity is a characteristic of the questing mind, roving widely in the search for new experiences that will cast light on life's meaning and purpose – as well as revealing its infinite wonders at all levels. The great scientists were systemically curious. Cultivate this quality in itself, asking questions of everyone you meet, in your constant search for broader and deeper knowledge and better understanding. The social level of questioning – "And what do you do?" – will only take you so far. Delve deeper and enrich yourself.

⊜ See yourself from outside

Stepping outside your own viewpoint and looking at yourself as others see you is difficult: it takes imagination and a willingness to confront difficult truths. But it's a useful exercise in improving self-knowledge. It has been said that the one thing we don't know about ourselves is the thing other people know only too well. See if you can find that grain of knowledge, or at least perception, outside yourself. Learn from it and act on your discovery.

⊜ Question norms

Our sense of what is the right thing to think, say or do in any situation is likely to be, in part, socially determined. Some of the great achievers and the great influencers have turned propriety on its head with revolutionary ideas that have changed the way we operate. Just think of how women and non-white races were regarded for much of history. Challenge the norms and see if they stand up to scrutiny. Ruffling feathers now and then might be exactly the right thing to do. Sometimes it is good to fly in the face of accepted norms.

⊜ Spark a word riot

Let your thinking go wild on paper. Marshalling your thoughts into words is a time-honoured means of self-expression, but to convey the nuances of what you think and feel can take practice and literary skill. Why not reserve a whole journal for a random splurge of words, expressing the contents of your mind without regard for grammar or cadence? If you wish, you can come back later and tease out individual strands of meaning, expressing them more conventionally. This is an excellent route towards self-knowledge.

ACTION PLAN

Moving towards
LIFELONG CALM

10 ACTION POINTS

➔ Give like the sun

However constrained your circumstances, you always have something to give – cash, food, support, assistance, reassurance, smiles. Make this your habit, in place of all the habits that are based on taking. Feel the moral and emotional benefits of generosity heighten your self-worth and suffuse you with peace.

➔ Offer your time and energy

Two of the most rewarding things you can give are your time and labour. Plenty of people around you will *need* to have jobs done for them – seek them out and offer your services. The elderly, in particular, have a tough time as they lose strength and mobility. The tasks you can usefully perform for others include housework, shopping, driving, decorating, gardening, childcare and dog walking. The nobility of voluntary labour adds to your karmic credit. Build charitable service into your life – even an hour a week, if that's all you can spare.

➔ Get involved

Having a say in local affairs is empowering. Your horizons as an individual citizen are broadened by involvement in the backroom decisions that affect your life and those of your neighbours. Immerse yourself in communal activism. Raise your voice on behalf of others. Shape the collective destiny you all share. This might require hard work but it's paradoxically relaxing to understand that you are making a difference.

➔ Ration digital life

All aspects of the internet – social media, online buying, info browsing – are potentially damaging when they start to impinge on quality analogue time. They encourage isolation. However connective they are for social sharing, online activities put a distance between yourself and others. Face-to-face meetings and phone calls are more empathic. Don't use your tablet or smartphone as a regular filler – a screensaver, as it were, to real life. Fill your downtime moments instead with unmediated life, even if it's only sitting in a café, reflecting or observing.

➲ Mindfully peel fruit

Directing all your attention to the sensory experience of peeling and eating, say, an orange is a typical procedure in mindfulness practice, which has become a runaway mind–body–spirit phenomenon. Mindfulness meditation can make us calmer and more focused, as well as enhancing physical well-being. The key ingredients are: living more in the moment, less in the past or future; recognizing emotions without getting caught up in them; and identifying the authentic you, rather than you as the sum of your feelings and mistakes (see pages 106–9).

➲ Pass through the pixel prism

We can't see ourselves as others do, but we *can* record ourselves on video, thanks to smartphones, tablets and digital cameras. Film yourself talking to a friend. Play back and fully acknowledge that this is you in action. Keep watching the clip until you're relaxed about the impression conveyed, forgiving any quirks or tics. Then ask yourself whether there's anything in the way you communicate that you'd like to change. Repeat the exercise now and then, until your self-image holds no surprises for you.

➲ Rise with the lark

The morning is a blessed time, and getting up early every day, and even earlier at least once a week, gives you the best chance of a peaceful day ahead. If you face challenges, you can mentally prepare for them, perhaps with a meditation. If the day is going to be routine, do something special before you enter the habitual flow – such as walking in the garden or reading a favourite poem.

➲ Declutter your home

Clutter is distracting – a perpetual reminder of a job on your to-do list. Tidy without delay to create a simplified environment that will bring more order to your life in a way that's subliminally relaxing. Discard superfluous items you are keeping as a way to hold on to the past.

➲ Keep and mend

We live in a throwaway society where it's easy to be spellbound by the flawless novelty of the pristine. This is materialism at its most insidious. Instead of listening to consumerism's siren call, keep faith with old possessions if they still serve their function. Does it matter if your old kitchen is beginning to look vintage? Could those socks be revived with darning? Spare a thought for our planet's groaning landfill sites. Materialism feeds on our weaknesses and undermines our peace.

➲ Champion the maligned

Critical carping is often heard from those who have no real understanding of what makes others tick. Often it springs from envy – or boredom. Make it your mission to correct the injustice of the thoughtless put-down. Enhance your self-esteem by standing up for open-mindedness and tolerance.

How to deal with
CHANGE
AND RISK

Uncertainty is a characteristic woven into any rewarding life — total predictability tends to be stultifying. Change often comes at us out of the blue, challenging our assumptions and calling upon us to show a range of qualities, including courage, resilience and flexibility. But any human life is also going to be punctuated by the changes we make ourselves — whether to escape undesirable circumstances, such as a boring job or a claustrophobic relationship, or to fulfil a strong intention to move towards a desirable future.

CHAPTER 3

"When the winds of change blow, some people build walls and other people build windmills."

CHINESE SAYING

To a great extent, peace of mind and happiness depend on our attitude to change, uncertainty and risk – a trio of related factors that occupy so much of our thinking. To translate this idea into more proactive terms, we need to exhibit decision-making and responsiveness – action and reaction. Both mental and emotional factors come into play as we navigate a world of infinite permutations, surfing change to turn it to our advantage or prevent it from overpowering us.

Seeing change
IN THE ROUND

Whether we strive for change or have it imposed upon us involuntarily, adapting to new circumstances can take flexibility, courage and resilience. Working to build these qualities in ourselves can usefully equip us to deal with the unexpected or to embark on any venture that involves risk.

"They must often change, who would be constant in happiness or wisdom," said Confucius. When we speak of being stuck in a groove, we often have a sense of missed opportunities or abandonment – of being left behind by the flow. There are many ways this can happen. We may cease to learn and grow, because we either have become complacent or find ourselves unable to escape a limiting environment. Sometimes we may feel outpaced by the speed of social or technological change, unable for some reason to keep up. In such instances we may not realize that the only solution would be for us to change, rather than for evolution to be reversed; or we may have this understanding, yet still find it impossible to modernize our ways.

Fear and risk
One of the factors that often makes change difficult to embrace is fear. We see change happening around us and yet we cling to the old order – despite the fact that it no longer rests on solid foundations. We may fear that we are not really capable of handling the change, or that we don't have the required resources to see it through to a happy conclusion. Only once we recognize and explode our own delusions can we break out of the prison of the past and move on.

This will often involve an element of risk, since considered risk is a necessary element in our striving for fulfilment. Ideally:

- The risk will stem from a deep-seated desire – so that taking it feels not like a gamble but more like a first step in an ambitious journey.
- Even if success is not achieved, the attempt will bring its own benefits – for example, self-knowledge, new contacts or new skills.
- Any losses will be foreseen and containable, and you will have contingency plans for dealing with them.

Threatening blue skies
When change sends shock waves our way, that is not necessarily because we do not expect it. However, being mentally prepared for something is not

the same as being emotionally immune. Emotions cannot be kept at bay by rationalization. This means that we all need, at certain times, to draw upon resilience and resourcefulness to ride the storm. It helps to have resilience already in place, as a personal reserve, and to some extent this can be achieved in advance by working on self-awareness and acceptance, perhaps through mindfulness meditation. Knowing and deeply accepting the reality of inevitable change, as Buddhists do in their understanding of suffering, can cushion us to some extent against the impact of loss or trauma.

Ourselves and others

Another aspect of acceptance is our appreciation of others as free agents whose wishes may not coincide with ours, even in a close relationship. Attempts to persuade or dissuade can only go so far. There is a risk of self-delusion if you imagine that the other person will eventually see things from your point of view. To believe this is often a failure of imagination. True empathy means acknowledging that none of us has the right to set tramlines for another's behaviour. Any attempt to do so will bring tension into our lives.

"To exist is to change, to change is to mature, to mature is to go on creating oneself endlessly."

HENRI BERGSON (1859–1941)

The art of
FLEXIBILITY

Mental and emotional flexibility amount to an excellent toolkit to put to use whenever we are facing change, whether self-generated or external. By responding nimbly to evolving circumstances, or a bolt out of the blue, we put ourselves in the best position to navigate the challenge most accurately.

Having too rigid a mindset can damage our prospects for well-being. Sometimes we are unable to respond nimbly to a situation. Instead, we seem destined to repeat our habitual reactions to circumstances in the past that have been broadly similar. In other words, we slip into the mode that therapists and psychologists often call "autopilot".

Autopilot reactions occur when a pattern of cause and effect has become deeply ingrained in our emotional make-up. Imagine you suffered stress at school because a callous teacher routinely humiliated you for your exam performance. This has led you to be deeply anxious when confronted by any kind of formal testing. Even twenty years later, every time you sit your driving test, you fail, even though you are competent at the wheel and well versed in the theory. Habitual emotions are hindering you from moving forwards and realizing your potential. This can happen in any area of life.

Autopilot emotional patterns often explain the following tendencies:

- ➲ **ADDICTIVE BEHAVIOUR** – when we use stimulation or desensitization (food, drink, drugs or gambling) repeatedly as escape routes from our problems, so that the habit becomes part of our lives.
- ➲ **AVOIDANCE OF RELATIONSHIP COMMITMENT** – based on our failed relationships in the past, and the hurt they have caused.
- ➲ **FAILURE TO ASSERT PERSONAL NEEDS** – when we seek to avoid confrontation because it has undermined our well-being in our previous experiences.

Habit breaking

The traditional strategy for breaking a habit is to frame a resolution – at the start of the New Year, for instance. However, this seldom achieves a lasting result, as the intention to change is not backed up by any real power. A more effective approach is to do some serious and mindful work on the emotional patterns within yourself, recognizing their symptoms, triggers and ultimate causes, and the fact that they are far from inevitable.

REACTIONS AND RESPONSES

Reactions take place when a trigger prompts us to behave automatically and emotionally, without spending any time thinking about the situation. Responses take place when intuition comes into play instead. A response, which tends to be slower and more considered than a reaction, is always likely to yield a more original and more satisfactory result. The basic differences are outlined in the following diagram. A flexible mind is characterized by complex responses rather than oversimplified reactions.

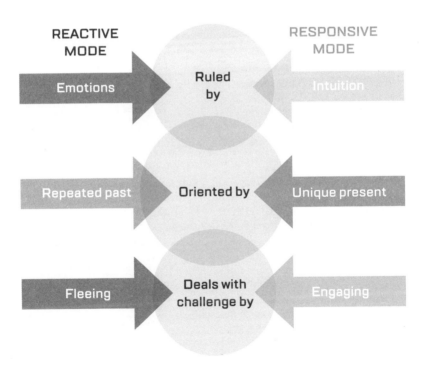

If you can apply intuitive wisdom to your situation, you will see that "autopilot" reactions can only happen if you give them your permission. Once you have reached this insight, you can start to build positive habits in place of the negative ones. Remember that simply trying to stop a bad habit is not enough: our unconscious mind does not understand a negative. Displacing the habit with a deeply felt positive intention – for example, to lose weight, get fit and be better able to help your aged father maintain his garden – is more effective. Go beyond the abstract to the concrete – imagine yourself doing specific things that are currently beyond you.

The self-analysis that precedes and prepares for habit-breaking can be painful – you need to confront your weaknesses unflinchingly. However, it's important not to be harsh on yourself. The optimum approach is to be objective in your observations and compassionate in your responses. Use your intuition to reach an understanding of how present patterns of reaction are harming you. Frame a plan for a healthier, happier life.

Flexible thinking

We often attempt to apply reason and intuition, rather than emotion, to make judgments and decisions – although, in fact, an emotional colouring to our conclusions may sometimes be hard to escape. Flexibility of mind has a number of ingredients, all of which should be cultivated:

- Willingness to consider all the factors without any preconceptions about the most valid conclusions we might reach.
- Openness to opinions different from our own – it may help if we are prepared to actively seek a whole range of views and sift them according to merit.
- Willingness to change our minds in the light of new evidence – or simply because further reflection has yielded a different result from what we originally thought.

When open-mindedness is taken to extremes, however, the result may be an inability to commit to a course of action. Such procrastination may have its ultimate origin in low self-esteem or self-confidence. As the decision-making moment draws near, we start getting anxious that we will make the wrong choice. This is a form of risk aversion, where anxiety about what might go wrong if we decide on particular course deters us from taking the critical decision.

Strategies for
CHANGE

When effecting change that is planned or undertaken willingly, we may be stressed by the loss of our familiar orientation points. We may also lose touch with our motivation or doubt whether the change we plan is possible, especially if it involves replacing a whole set of deep-rooted habits. However, there are various strategies and approaches we can draw on to make the change process more reliable and more enriching.

When initiating and travelling through change, intuition will usually be your invaluable inner compass. Objective reason will often be incapable of resolving your dilemmas. Where there's a choice of many pathways, each with its own array of possible outcomes, pure reason tends not to be adequate for confident decision-making.

Reason, emotion and intuition

At times of change your emotions are likely to come into play, and your apparently rational thinking might be coloured by them. Intuition may then work as a useful check on your reasoning. It's a familiar experience: you decide on a course of action, but then an inner voice deters you at the last moment. Intuition kicks in, thank goodness, to apply an emergency brake.

Listening to positive intuitive messages can be more difficult than detecting the negative ones. You need to learn how your intuition communicates with you. There are times when its subtle messaging is drowned out by "noise". This can include any evidence you are amassing, the advice you are given and your own anxieties. Finding a quiet place where you can tune in to any intuitive signals can help.

Deep change

When we opt to make changes within the fluid realm of personality and lifestyle – changes in our attitudes, responses and habits – it can be difficult to answer the question "How should I go about this?" We might even believe that personality is a fixity of our life, something we are stuck with, determined perhaps by heredity and upbringing.

As a corrective to this pessimistic idea about the prospects of self-development, think for a moment about how a bad habit forms. There has to be a first time it happens – the first time you ran away from a relationship or the first time you sought refuge in empty distractions, or worse. Habits are not intrinsic, even if you can trace their roots back to childhood. They stem from emotions, which you can experience without acting on them – this is one of the insights of mindfulness. If you can allow habits to form, you can reverse them, changing your behaviour – your reaction to the emotion in question – by a conscious decision to which you are fully committed.

Here is a step-by-step strategy for effecting a deep personal change:

1 Confront the damaging effects of what it is you wish to eliminate from your life.

How to make a
LARGE-SCALE CHANGE

Making a big change that has repercussions in different areas of life can be daunting and stressful. It will call upon your self-belief, your staying power, your decisiveness and sometimes your courage. Here are some guidelines to give yourself the best chance of success:

》 To diminish the perceived enormity of a big change in your life circumstances, break the change down into small segments, treating each one as a separate undertaking.

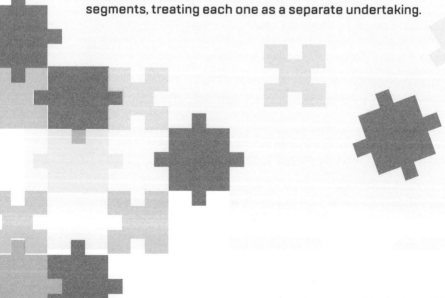

2 Visualize the positive benefits of replacing bad habits by good.

3 Formulate intentions to bring this transformation into effect.

4 Whenever you detect an emotion or urge you know will be unproductive if you react to it habitually, step back from it and observe it mindfully, without judgment.

5 Activate your new response and relish the benefits you know it will bring you.

6 Celebrate your success in breaking the negative pattern of emotion that leads to habitual reaction.

≫ To help to reduce the stress of change, be sociable. Share what you are going through with others and seek reassurance or guidance from them, based on their experiences.

≫ Try to see your big change as an adventure – one that will take you into new territory and allow you to make discoveries en route about who you are and what you can become.

≫ Stay connected with your motivation – it can be inspiring to visualize the benefits that the change will bring. Remind yourself of those benefits frequently.

≫ Be prepared for the unfolding outcome to look different from what is in your mind's eye – life is more richly complex than you can predict and, if things don't go exactly according to your vision, that's neither surprising nor necessarily undesirable.

≫ Create order within the flux as an anchor that can give you reassurance – change can be messy, and it can be beneficial to set up some tidy structures within the process, even if they are only provisional.

Calm approaches
TO RISK

To remain indefinitely within our zone of familiarity, even if it were possible, would be a sad way to lead a life. The sense of better experiences out there, of opportunities missed, would eventually start to nag away at our peace of mind. To move towards fulfilment inevitably involves some risk-taking.

Perceiving the level of risk we face will all too often deter us from embarking on potentially beneficial changes. If we seek fulfilment, we need to cultivate a healthy attitude to risk – one characterized by awareness (understanding what we are doing) combined with open-heartedness and courage (relishing the challenge).

Permutations of response

When a risk is perceived, there are four possible ways of dealing with it:

1 ACCEPT You decide that the benefits outweigh the risks and embark on your adventure. It's sensible to do this only after considering first whether taking the second way ("reduce") is possible.

2 REDUCE You decide to limit the level of risk. One way to do this might be to ensure that the change you plan proceeds in modest stages, so that you can backtrack more easily at any point, if necessary. Or, if there are a number of possible changes, you decide on the one change that is the least risky.

3 TRANSFER This is an unlikely choice in most situations. If you are embarking on a business venture, transferring the risk might involve finding a backer. At the personal level, we tend to be solely responsible for the changes we make. When acting as a couple, however, the sense of being in a new situation together can make it easier to deal with.

4 AVOID This involves either continuing to accept the status quo or looking for a safer way of changing it.

Making bold changes is often the way to become the self we want to be, living the life that gives us the best chances of realizing our potential. On the other hand, these changes are less likely to be fruitful if they don't stem from

THE RISK
questionnaire

**When considering taking a risk – anything from
moving home to investing time and money in an expensive
personal project – ask yourself the following questions** (given
here with guidelines to help you answer them or make use of the answers):

Is the risk you are contemplating normal for its context?
(There is nothing surprising about the risks an entrepreneur takes, or the decision
to train for a new skill, or to enter a new relationship)

Does the risk concern you alone or will it impact on others, too?
(If the latter, you need to involve them in decision-making if possible)

Is the only downside the waste of time and energy?
(If so, perhaps you will find the attempt rewarding and instructive. At least you
will not end up with a sense of missed opportunity)

Will perceived failure involve the loss of much that you currently value?
(If so, ask yourself what the impact of that loss will be and weigh it carefully
against the benefit. Exercise caution, but be prepared to accept some losses)

**If you are reluctant to take the risk, is it your intuitive wisdom or your
risk aversion that is warning you against it?**
(Risk aversion is a habit you might choose to overcome, but we ignore intuition
at our peril)

**Will you discuss the risk with others or just to go ahead without
making a fuss?**
(Going public is a good way to test your decision-making, but it is wise to come
to a provisional conclusion first)

Is your current situation a source of fulfilment, despite its frustrations?
(If so, consider whether to work on the frustrations, and leave the situation
broadly intact)

Are you bored with the familiar and ready for a challenge?
(Consider what aspects of the familiar you would ideally hang on to. Perhaps you
can have it both ways)

a promising inner foundation – a mental and emotional flexibility, an openness to the new, and a willingness to make mistakes and learn from them.

Any external changes you put in train should ideally work hand in hand with internal changes. Although you might at times opt to make an external change to *force* yourself to be more flexible, this itself carries risks, and you should make sure that you are not overstretching yourself when making one giant leap.

Embracing failure

Fear of failure motivates many of us not to accept a risk we might be entertaining. But what does failure mean? In assessing the stakes involved in taking a risk for positive change, it's better to think in terms of potential loss rather than failure. In the neuro-linguistic programming (NLP) approach to psychological therapy, there's no such thing as failure – only feedback. The notion that failure is inherently shameful is profoundly misguided, though sadly commonplace. There's no loss in, for example, being turned down. We should also bear in mind that moving in one direction and not reaching the imagined destination is an experience that contributes to our growth.

"To dare is to lose one's footing momentarily. Not to dare is to lose oneself."

SØREN KIERKEGAARD (1813–1855)

Powering
CHANGE

We have assessed the risks and have decided to take the plunge. How do we ensure that we keep up the impetus for change once we have determined our course of action? How do we prevent the change momentum from losing energy and reverting back to inaction?

Having a clear vision for change sounds like good advice – the kind we might read about in business self-help books. In fact, a *clear* vision tends to be something of a luxury. We are more likely to perceive our desired outcome dimly, since the future is a blank page on which a legible text will form only once we are some distance into our change journey.

The poetry of change

The creativity metaphor is appropriate, since what we are doing is applying creativity to the elements of our own life. It can be inspiring to think of yourself as scripting your change as you go along, like a poet writing a poem. The following factors come into play in both activities:

- No precise knowledge of the end result until completion – yet an approximate idea of the desired outcome provides motivation.
- Willingness to make false starts and begin again as soon as uncorrectable weaknesses are apparent.
- Being prepared to set off down byways that may lead nowhere, making it necessary to go back to the fork in the road and take another route.
- Openness to being pleasantly surprised by twists and turns in the path.
- Seizing chances opportunistically as they occur.
- Satisfaction at being involved in a creative process.
- Knowing that revisions can and may need to be made to the final outcome, once you have lived with it for a while – even small revisions can be transformative.

Maintaining motivation

Once you have started to effect change, keeping faith is essential if the initial impetus is not to dissipate. This means staying close to your motivation. Think of this motivation in personified form, as your best possible self, who has inspired your initial resolution. Visit this optimum self often in your imagination. Allow yourself to be responsive to a pep talk from that self.

Some might find it more effective to be inspired instead by a talismanic object, perhaps something small you can carry in your pocket or your handbag. Some possibilities might be:

- **A MINERAL EGG** This can be found in shops that sell crystals. You can draw on the energy of the egg, which has symbolic associations with a new start.
- **A FOREIGN COIN** The foreign origin reflects the fact that you have committed to entering exciting new territory.
- **A PEBBLE FROM A BEACH** The analogy is that you are sailing an unknown ocean; the pebble denotes the shore of the promised land.

Once you have acquired your talisman, hold it in your palm and contemplate it, thinking about your reason for change and your commitment to the process. Visualize the energy of your will to change absorbing into the talisman, so it becomes invested in that energy. Afterwards, carry your talisman with you at all times and use it in the following motivational exercise, daily or weekly, or whenever your impetus for change is flagging.

1 Hold the talisman in your palm and gaze at it while you imagine yourself drawing its energy through both your arm and your eye, until it has suffused your whole self with the commitment to continue.

2 If you need a short break from the change process, put the talisman on a windowsill, where it can draw energy from sunlight. But mark on your calendar or in your diary when you plan to take up the process again, and honour this intention.

"I am always doing that which I cannot do, in order that I may learn how to do it."

PABLO PICASSO (1881–1973)

Overcoming obstacles
TO CHANGE

Listed here are some common obstacles that may well place themselves on your path from time to time, together with the commitments you need to formulate in order to overcome these barriers.

If you wish, you can express your commitment as an affirmation: "I commit to trusting …", and so on. Hold your talisman in your hand (see opposite) as you make your affirmation.

STRESS
Put your problems in perspective and reduce the stress by mindful detachment from your anxieties.

DISTRACTION
Say "no" to competing demands on your time, while continuing to fulfil your responsibilities, perhaps with help from others.

CRITICISM
Trust your own judgment and intuition.

SELF-DOUBT
Take a positive view of your abilities, based on the knowledge that your doubt stems from habitual thinking rooted in the past.

FATIGUE
Commit to renewed effort after suitable rest or refreshment.

Coping with
SHOCKS

We know that no life is immune to sudden reversals of fortune, and that bereavement, and probably illness, will impact on us all. However, when a shock befalls us, no amount of theoretical preparation will make the impact any easier to cope with. Here are some guidelines for dealing with any shock likely to result in emotional turbulence.

When an earthquake destroys a village, or fire rampages through a tower block, the residents, as disaster strikes, are probably worrying about other things entirely, such as how to pay their rent or how to find someone to look after the kids tomorrow. They may simply be asleep. Sometimes, as with a flood, there's a warning – you see the river rising, allowing you a little time to build up defences. Even so, the impact can be devastating.

Loss and grief run their painful course, with each victim walking their own path of suffering. One consolation of communal shock is that it brings people together, providing a setting in which compassion and selflessness can shine.

The personal dimension

Although similar scenarios cannot be ruled out, shock, in our own lives, is likely to take a narrower, more individual form – accident, bereavement or diagnosis. Shock inevitably prompts a swirl of emotions, and it's beneficial to recognize them as they happen – and forgive yourself for them. The mix will probably include:

- **NUMBNESS** A sense of being in a daze is a frequent reaction to shocking news. You may not be able to hear what people are saying.
- **SADNESS** This can seem overwhelming, with prolific tears. You might find yourself trying not to cry, in case you find it impossible to stop.
- **FATIGUE** The effort of processing difficult knowledge and trying to still the emotional storm can be draining. Yet sleep may elude you.
- **ANGER** When affected by the loss or illness of someone close, you may feel anger towards them or God, or both. Any shock may make you lash out after a minor upset.
- **GUILT** You may feel guilty about being angry, or about your own inability to prevent what happened.

"Sadness flies on the wings of the morning and out of the heart of darkness comes the light."

JEAN GIRAUDOUX (1882–1944)

FOUR STAGES OF SHOCK

After a shock or trauma, even a relatively low-level one such as failing exams unexpectedly, we can expect to go through the following stages. It can help to identify them as they happen. Knowing what stage you are going through instils the sense that you will eventually be able to move on.

1 ACCEPTANCE
It can take time to accept that the loss or disappointment is real – you might find yourself waking up and then suddenly remembering.

2 EMOTIONAL AFTERMATH
The emotions may keep surfacing long after the event. If you have suffered from low self-esteem, this might well return for a while.

3 ADJUSTMENT
In time, you will find ways to accommodate yourself to the new reality. You will establish new routines and start to resume old ones that you have neglected.

4 RECOVERY
You probably cannot recover what you have lost, but you can recover positivity and optimism, and summon the energy for something new – in other words, you can move on.

Each individual is different, and you should not be surprised if your emotions and, even more likely, your behavioural reactions strike you as puzzling or bizarre. Often people in shock forget things – you might leave the gas on when cooking, or go outside in winter without your coat. In the immediate aftermath of a disaster, it's pointless wasting energy trying to keep the lid on your emotions. Give them space, trying as best you can to continue with your life. Forgive yourself for any eruptions – others will understand.

A normal front

Don't be surprised if you find yourself surprisingly capable in some areas. You might feel able and keen to work as normal or meet friends, though even when busy you may feel alone or lost deep down. In bereavement, strangely, you might have moments of euphoria. It's possible you will make some ambitious plans, and even take steps to put them into effect, only later realizing they are unsuitable. Beware of signing up to inappropriate commitments during this vulnerable period.

Lesser shocks

When we are preoccupied with our own concerns, even lesser shocks – such as losing a wedding ring or being diagnosed with a serious but not life-threatening illness – can give rise to high levels of sadness and anxiety that undermine our inner peace. A lifestyle in which giving and compassion are major strands, alongside mindfulness, may cushion us against this kind of setback, by making it more likely that we will see our problems in a broader context. Making an inventory of what good fortune has brought our way may reveal more reasons for celebration than unhappiness.

"Those who don't know how to weep with their whole heart don't know how to laugh either."

GOLDA MEIR (1898–1978)

Building
RESILIENCE

Resilience is the quality that keeps us intact and optimistic when we are buffeted by bad luck and disappointment, which all of us are sure to encounter at various times in our lives. Being resilient gives us the best possible protection from the troublesome aspects of change, whether we choose that change or have it imposed upon us by external forces.

Resilience is a quality we build through practice. The journey of change will inevitably help us to develop it. With time and experience, we learn we can cope with whatever the journey brings.

Being able to take big changes in our stride is an enviable gift. When we find ourselves wobbled off course by change, so that it engages our emotions and calls for our coping strategies to be brought into play, that's usually because we have become accustomed to a stable, predictable mode of living. Indeed, we may have come to see that stability as a reliably rigid structure, allowing us to grow habits upon it – like ivy clinging to a trellis.

In reality, no structure or method of organization remains as fixed as it might seem. Just think of the instability of business, where the ups and downs of the economy might force a firm to make changes to staff numbers. People move on, by choice or involuntarily – not only from jobs but also from family and friends, and even from intimate relationships that to an outsider, or even one of the participants, might seem unshakable.

The quality that most helps us to weather these and other kinds of unwanted change is resilience, which may be defined as an ability to adapt well to unplanned circumstances.

Mutability

A sound philosophical basis for resilience might be the acceptance that life is, as Shakespeare or any of his contemporaries might have said, "mutable" – that is, intrinsically liable to change. However, accepting

"Our greatest glory is not in never falling, but in rising every time we fall."
CONFUCIUS (551–479 BCE)

RECIPE FOR resilience

There are aspects of ourselves we can work on if we seek to
be more resilient. The following list provides a useful starting
point for self-inquiry. Work through it and score yourself
out of ten on each quality. After a month of working on your
self-awareness, flexibility and mindful detachment from your
emotions, and replacing bad habits with good, score yourself
again to see how far you have progressed.

》 Being aware of change as a defining feature of life

first score ☐   second score ☐

》 Flexibility of mind and emotions

first score ☐   second score ☐

》 Ensuring the plans you make are realistic

first score ☐   second score ☐

》 Being positive about life

first score ☐   second score ☐

》 Communicating well with yourself and others

first score ☐   second score ☐

》 Learning lessons from experience

first score ☐   second score ☐

》 Attending mindfully to your emotions

first score ☐   second score ☐

》 Knowing how to deal effectively with stress

first score ☐   second score ☐

》 Being a good decision-maker

first score ☐   second score ☐

a truth hypothetically is very different from *feeling* that truth, at a deep level of awareness. To feel the reality of mutability, we need to have experienced it. The following factors may help us to come to the required level of felt understanding:

- Not being straitjacketed by habitual emotions and the behaviour that springs from them. If we start to break our habitual patterns of living, we become more resilient to change in general.
- Understanding the forces that operate on our life situations. This is largely a matter of understanding context. For example, if we know more about the health difficulties our son's wife's aged parents are having, the easier it becomes for us to accept the couple's decision to move house to live nearer to them as part-time carers. Resilience may be strengthened by knowledge of the causes that shape our circumstances.
- Having experience of risk-taking. Leading the safest of possible lives is poor preparation for change. Risk-takers learn to be more adaptable.

Bend like bamboo

The Japanese traditionally see the flexibility of bamboo as an optimum model for human behaviour. Being too rigid in our responses makes us susceptible to shattering. To bend whichever way the wind blows ensures that our well-being is more likely to be maintained.

Resilient people believe in themselves and their ability to manage challenges successfully. Moreover, such individuals are usually more proactive and are more likely to take steps to prevent particular problems from occurring.

"The world breaks everyone, and afterward, some are strong at the broken places."

ERNEST HEMINGWAY (1899–1961)

Accepting the
UNKNOWN

It's impossible to know the future. All we can do is set an intention, move in our chosen direction and be prepared to respond to, and ideally to relish, the encounters we have along the way – with people, with circumstances and with qualities of our own selves that we cannot know until they are brought into play.

However energetic we are in seeking knowledge about ourselves, our circumstances and our prospects, there are bound to be things that remain a closed book to us. The main unknowns in most situations can be summarized as follows (with statements suggesting why these factors need not be a cause for anxiety):

THE FUTURE
- Future events
- Future outcomes

(The future is not a concrete situation – only the medium of your fulfilment – and therefore it's not to be feared.)

OTHER PEOPLE
- What they will do
- How they will respond to us

(Unless you make a specific effort to influence others, they will follow their own course – the key thing is not what they do but how you respond to it.)

OURSELVES
- Our level of success
- Our responses to new situations

(If you commit to a good intention and respond well to challenges, there will be no real failure – your responses to any situation are within your control.)

When contemplating the future, all you have to rely on to sketch in its features is your imagination. If you have low self-esteem or low levels of confidence, this will prompt you to imagine bad outcomes. The result is stasis or lack of growth – you stay where you are. Accepting the blank future, with all its unknowns, as exciting rather than threatening tends to be a self-generating experience, preparing the ground for a harvest of fulfilment.

A world of others

Our encounters with others are the heartbeat of a shared planet and the essence of a rewarding life. At some point we are likely to experience love's inner blossoming. We will love family and friends, too; and if we can open our hearts, we will love humanity.

What we value about others is precisely that they are not ourselves. They have an endless capacity to surprise. Our future will be populated by people we need to interact with, some of whom we have met already – what is unknown is how they will respond to us. Some of our interactions will involve disagreement, even conflict. This must be accepted, just as you accept the possibility of rain or cold winds.

It's healthy to think of such challenges not as conflict, which implies a winner and a loser, but as creative interaction. Resilience and flexibility give you the best chance to emerge from your encounters without any sense of failure or regret, even if you experience disappointment.

The unknown within

Since our own qualities and potential are so complex, we have an infinite capacity for surprising *ourselves*. The basic rules for dealing with surprise are simple:

1 When you fall short of your hopes or expectations, accept the situation, forgive yourself, learn from the experience and move on.

2 When you exceed your hopes or expectations, celebrate success and upwardly revise your evaluation of your own potential.

3 When you are not surprising yourself either way, maybe you are in a rut? Start making plans at once.

Self-development is never a matter of working towards a one-size-fits-all model of personal qualities. It will always involve self-exploration, which means prospecting your own depths. This may not be where your treasure chests lie, but it's where you will find the keys.

"People wish to be settled; only as far as they are unsettled is there any hope for them."

RALPH WALDO EMERSON (1803–1882)

Byways of
CHANGE

Having set a change in motion, or committed to making the best of an imposed change, you will find plenty of learning opportunities as you go. You will also encounter new experiences that are likely to make your journey worthwhile, whatever its ultimate outcome.

If you see change as simply a matter of progressing from A to B, you are taking a narrow and unnecessarily impoverishing view. It's true that, if you are responding to trauma or loss, just keeping yourself afloat for a while might be all you can manage. But when the change is undertaken voluntarily for self-development reasons, or revolves around practicalities such as job or home, there's often much to be gained from the change *journey*, wherever that takes you in the end.

Fellow travellers

Many change adventures involve meeting new people, who may be incidental to your intention but nevertheless can teach you something valuable, extend your horizons or offer you some kind of perhaps unexpected insight or satisfaction. If the change requires you to train for a new skill, you may come across a mentor who can teach you other things as well. Anyone who happens to be sharing your journey, or crossing your path, can be invaluable as a source of inspiring perspectives. Remember, too, the simple fact that meeting new people is the self-evident way to make new friends; when you are moving in new directions and shaking up your routines, friendships can blossom easily.

Because we are a sociable species, there will usually be, in any new undertaking, opportunities to relax and share leisure time with others. Even if your intention is nothing more than to abandon unhealthy habits and lose a few pounds at the gym, you will probably find fellow members who are happy to talk. Anyone committed to realizing their potential and finding fulfilment will appreciate the need for quality time spent on their own personal interests, and it's a short step from there to sharing a particular pursuit with others. It can be inspiring, too, to converse with people who are pursuing their own passions, and you may soon feel like having a go yourself, whether at bookbinding, aromatherapy or synchronized swimming.

Byways beckon

If, during change, we can see, and open ourselves up to, a range of new possibilities, we start to arrive at a new definition – not moving from A to B but moving from A *towards* B, with an eye to C, D and E, as well. The box below illustrates the fluidity of the change journey when it's undertaken with the minimum of preconceptions.

The idea of narrow determination and focus as prerequisites of success is outmoded, even in the business world, where measurable results are all-important. It's more productive to embark on change with 360-degree vision, in a spirit of freestyle experiment, with a willingness to be distracted from any preformulated purpose. If what comes out of the process is the decision to go back to school, spend a year in a Tibetan monastery or set up a charitable foundation for the victims of nursing home abuse, so be it. Even staying where you were, but with greater appreciation of how that can bring positive benefits, can be a winning outcome from a quest for something different.

CHANGE PATHWAYS

Any change journey will take you to forks in the road where you would do well to weigh all the options. Remember, you will usually be able to retrace your steps if you feel you have taken the wrong turn. Also, even spurs off the main track should be explored if they seem interesting. You might decide to alter your ultimate goal in the light of exploring one of these new pathways.

You start by following the intended path of change but then:

● At a fork in the road you decide to deviate in an unplanned direction.

OR

● While exploring a spur off the intended path, you decide to follow it as your main way forwards.

THOUGHT PLAN

Changing your
PERSPECTIVE

3 AFFIRMATIONS

➡ "I relish the refurbishment of my world – the replacement of old with new."

➡ "I commit to change without becoming anxious or obsessed. As I strive, life's values and satisfactions all remain available."

➡ "My mind is a miraculous engine, giving me the strength and flexibility to transform myself."

7 THOUGHT POINTS

➡ Survey your choices

Once you have decided to replace restrictive habits or routines with something new, you will no doubt need to consider a whole range of possible choices before committing to a particular experiment. Consider these choices with relish, as if looking from a height onto a new landscape you have discovered. Survey the terrain as a whole before deciding where to pitch camp for further exploration. Think of yourself as a pioneer, charting a new course through a land rich in possibilities. There are always choices that seem hidden because of mental beliefs and filters – aim to find at least one and, if possible, three.

➡ Allow time for insights

Intuition and instinct are different things. Instinct gives us an immediate reaction to a situation – often an instant feeling of attraction or recoil. Intuition, on the other hand, draws upon deep self-knowledge over a period of time. It can take days or even weeks for its messages to surface. Sleeping on a problem or a dilemma makes it more likely that intuition will deliver its insights, but allowing a few days is even better. You may even gain further intuitive understanding over a week or so.

● Confirm your intuition

Intuition gives excellent guidance, as if speaking from a mysterious inner oracle. Ponder its message and attempt to frame it to yourself in words, to see if it makes any kind of sense at the logical level. This will be an instance of rationalizing after the fact, but the process is useful as a means of confirmation. Sometimes putting your intuition into words will highlight possible flaws in your thinking that will prompt you to ponder a little longer.

● Risk time and energy

Before you take a risk, you will naturally evaluate exactly what you are staking. However, when you commit to replacing an unsatisfactory lifestyle with a more positive mode of living, the stakes will simply be your energy and time. Since the risk will inevitably bring you new experiences and new insights, not least into yourself, this kind of gamble is one you can hardly lose. There will often be an "opportunity cost" – the alternative course that's no longer available – but only economists worry about such things. Just move forwards with self-belief.

● Put money in perspective

There are countless ways in which change can use up cash. If you plan (or are forced) to leave a job, you may need to think up inventive ways to support yourself. Also, there's the possible cost of any new adventure – you might need to fund a course of education or training, or buy a boat or a piano. It helps to develop a healthy and expansive attitude to money. When you need to dip into savings, do so knowing there can be no better use of wealth than creating a better life for yourself. Money issues come with the territory when you follow your passion. Hold money in your head, but never in your heart.

● Question the plateau

Given that change is the essence of life, security is often illusory. We might imagine we have reached a plateau of routine and satisfaction, and can live there indefinitely, but "indefinitely" makes no sense in the context of a life's journey. Helen Keller said, "Security is mostly a superstition." Question your apparent fixities. Your values and best qualities will endure, if you stay true to them, but it's healthy to accept that your circumstances will change. Do all you can to ensure that you are mentally and emotionally prepared.

● Make your own decisions

Friends or family might be sceptical about your ability to make or use change effectively in your life, and some might try to alter your course – perhaps urging the safest option. Consider their concerns, but don't allow these well-wishers to take even a small fraction of the decision on your behalf. The only people whose views you may need to build into your decision-making are those who will take the journey with you – most probably your partner.

ACTION PLAN

Steering through CHANGE

10 ACTION POINTS

➔ Start a change journal

It's invaluable to record the change process, monitoring every stage to assess how things are going. Write down your decisions and responses. Use the journal, too, for noting affirmations – if you choose a pocket-sized book, this may make the affirmations more accessible when you need them. Sketch out timelines for change and create any mind maps you think might be helpful. If the journal becomes untidy, with lots of quick jottings, that's fine, as this reflects the often messy reality of change.

➔ Communicate your choices well

Keep your friends and loved ones well informed about your decisions. But speak of your intentions only if you have committed to them, since not following through may undermine credibility. If you have unresolved dilemmas, by all means share these with select individuals, but choose carefully. Not all friends will want a step-by-step commentary on your inner life – better, with some, just to have fun.

➔ Show empathy

When telling people about a change that will impact on their lives, be tactful and compassionate. This is usually desirable no matter how well you know the person. Try to see things from the other person's perspective. Listen to and engage with what they say. If someone will be disadvantaged or upset by a change, it's usually fairer not to tell them until you decisively opt for it – unless you intend to take their reaction into account before deciding.

➔ Take stock frequently

Set aside time at intervals to assess how your change is progressing. Make your assessment not just in terms of narrow goals but also looking at the broader context of how you feel life is going. Is the change generating any emotions you need to deal with? What have you discovered about yourself since your last assessment? Do you need to adjust your chosen direction? Be sure to celebrate achievements – obstacles overcome, lessons learned, people won over.

Stay fresh

Emotional fatigue can creep up on us unawares, so don't let your change project take over every cranny of your life. Ensure you have plenty of variety in your day and take regular breaks – to do stretching or breathing exercises, for example. Also, don't shut yourself off from your usual sources of stimulation. It can help to have one or two mini-projects running alongside the big change project – something as simple as refurbishing a flowerbed or taking part in a book group.

Use the language of peace

War metaphors permeate the world of business and seep into everyday life: "We declared a truce"; "I shot down all his arguments." This is not the best kind of language to support flexible thinking about self-development. We can conquer problems, but it's healthier to think in terms of negotiating them. It makes sense to avoid a way of speaking that encourages us to see every failure as a defeat.

Show gratitude

When preoccupied and perhaps even stressed by change, it's easy to neglect life's civilities. We may feel we don't have time to chat, but this means we don't have time to treat others as we would normally like to be treated ourselves. Many people are likely to help you, often unwittingly, in your change journey, and unless you go out of your way to thank them it may be that you are taking them for granted.

Cultivate *sprezzatura*

Sprezzatura is an Italian word meaning "nonchalance". It signifies a kind of graceful restraint, an ability to do tricky things without apparent effort. The quality stems from being at ease in your own skin and having confidence in your actions. Work at your self-esteem and your confidence, and you will notice that *sprezzatura* comes naturally to you in certain situations. It's a useful quality in the change process, when effort may often be all too visible.

Follow the 80–20 rule

Once you have decided what to do, the 80–20 rule, borrowed from the world of business, comes into play. The rule states that successful efforts are made up of 80 per cent follow-through on planned actions and 20 per cent planning for success. Follow-through is placed first (reversing the obvious chronological order) because of its importance. Remember this when you feel your motivation flagging.

Adopt a student mindset

We all know how keen students operate: making notes on lectures, consciously absorbing lessons, using clipboards to carry notes around. When learning new skills, or being induced into new procedures or situations, approach the process with the serious focus that a committed student would bring to bear. Don't just listen and remember. Make notes, revise, ask questions and show keenness.

How to stay calm
IN TOUGH TIMES

However resilient and resourceful we are, there are periods when we will be seriously tested. Ageing brings its particular challenges – impairments to our health and fitness, loss of loved ones and possibly retirement – even for those who initially feel prepared for it. But, at any age, new misfortunes can block the flow of normal life and threaten our peace of mind. Sometimes, we feel lost in turbulence, like a cork on a stormy sea. Circumstances pull us in different directions. Answering one challenge may call upon so much inner resilience and resource that fractures appear elsewhere in our lives – for example, in our ability to carry on working.

CHAPTER 4

"I ask not for a lighter burden,
but for broader shoulders."

JEWISH PROVERB

There are no easy ways to stay calm when events seem
to be conspiring against us. We need to allow ourselves
our emotional reactions and our inner turbulence, while
also reminding ourselves of core values that will hopefully
provide helpful orientation points. We need, as well, to
try to avoid certain pitfalls, such as feelings of
victimization. Most storms can be weathered and,
meanwhile, we can take comfort from the authenticity
of our response, and from the love of those around us,
which we must never take for granted.

Inner
TURBULENCE

When times turn tough, the mind often roams unproductively over its problems. A settled picture of the situation eludes us, since our view is obscured by emotions. Some common reactions to major challenges – anything from a relationship breakdown to a worrying diagnosis – are given here in general terms.

Imagine everyone's misfortunes, including yours, bundled together into one big heap. If you were instructed to select your own bundle of misfortunes rather than choose those of another, you might do so without much resistance, for two reasons. First, you would probably see bundles much larger than yours – those of people living through war or drought, or in a country without basic freedoms. In such places, there's more scope for misfortune to have an impact. You would also, no doubt, see bigger bundles awaiting many of your neighbours. Yours might be bigger than average, but some, certainly, would be bigger still.

Second, the notion of swapping your life for someone else's is philosophically meaningless. You might wish you were, say, Beyoncé; but Beyoncé exists, and if you could somehow become absorbed into the singer, her life would still be exactly as it is now. The only thing that would change is that you, as the person you have been, would no longer exist.

It's similarly delusional simply to wish that things were different. Wishing never makes anyone feel better, and indeed often highlights the impact of the problem rather than allowing you to move through it with positive intention.

Better or worse

Such thoughts may seem rather abstract, but when misfortune hits us hard we do tend to think in terms of a *somewhat* larger perspective. We might compare our lot with that of others, and look regretfully or even enviously in their direction – which can soon shade into pointless wishing. We might also look back to a happier past – the norm we were living before the current phase of challenge began. Again, there's delusion here, since life's norms have no lasting authority, but merely reflect how things were for a particular time. The emotional impact of current difficulties may include feelings of being treated unfairly by fate and nostalgia for happier times. Don't be too hard on yourself for such feelings, but do see them for what they are and opt instead for a flexible, positive response to your problems. It's the choices you make, rather than the emotions you feel, that will enable you to move forwards.

A MAP OF DARK PLACES

The following chart identifies emotions that tough times commonly instil in us. The emotions on the left are best addressed by working mindfully on your inner landscape – stepping aside from your emotions, regarding them with detachment and making concrete resolutions that will have the effect of displacing them. Those on the right lend themselves to more practical approaches.

DENIAL
Common initially
Positive response:
✔ Allow time to subside

ANGER
Common phase after denial
Positive response:
✔ Allow time to subside

BAFFLEMENT
The "Why me?" syndrome
Positive response:
✔ Displace by positive action; ask better-quality questions

HOPELESSNESS
Pessimism about the outcome
Positive response:
✔ Displace by positive action

ENTRAPMENT
All-consuming problems
Positive response:
Cultivate self-care ✔

ISOLATION
Less time with friends or family
Positive response:
Prioritize connections ✔

EXHAUSTION
Physically, mentally and emotionally overstretched
Positive response:
Cultivate self-care ✔

HELPLESSNESS
Feeling ineffective
Positive response:
Mobilize help; build self-esteem ✔

Accepting
THE PAIN

Some problems are so overwhelming we find ourselves unable to move beyond their shadow. Better to face your difficulties than try to deny or escape them. Battling against reality, like all inner fights, will be tiring and ultimately unproductive. Making peace with the situation – letting go of the thought of how unhappy it's making you – allows you to learn and adapt.

When we are deeply upset about something, we tend to kick back against the situation mentally and emotionally, and it's this struggle against uncomfortable reality that converts pain into distress. Some Buddhists describe this pattern of reaction as a formula:

PAIN × RESISTANCE = SUFFERING

One common form that such resistance might take is rejecting the reality of our emotions. Imagine a couple resisting the anger they feel towards each other. They experience not only the anger, which does not go away, but an inner conflict about that anger – an attempt to deny or suppress the emotion.

When serious misfortune strikes, a similar but more extreme kind of struggle will take place. You might resist the pain caused by, say, being made redundant, or the loss of someone you love, and in the process you end up creating your own suffering. The healthier response is to accept your authentic self with all its emotional reactions. Self-acceptance and self-compassion are key.

By facing a problem, rather than denying it in a way that brings suffering, we can move towards accommodating ourselves to its reality. When an experience is painful, we can seek a way to comfort ourselves and negotiate our predicament with the best possibility of a more tolerable outcome.

The idea of accepting emotions without believing they are who we are – without, as it were, being drawn into their story – is a key principle of mindfulness.

Spaces within suffering

To suffer is to experience the unhappiness that stems from physical or emotional pain, or both. In practice, our suffering often gets extended beyond the period when the pain is felt. Imagine you are upset when reminded of a loss – a house you loved, say. The new house, which you dislike, has a beautiful garden. When you sit there in warm sunshine, you can be potentially at peace. Yet the pain of losing the old house leaps forwards to fill your garden interlude. Suffering, by its own momentum, colonizes our neutral space.

The mindful approach in this situation would be to focus on the present moment as much as you can – to look at the trees, flowers and foliage, the insects buzzing around. Unhappy thoughts contrasting the new house with the old pass through your mind from time to time, but when this happens you return your focus to the garden, without judging yourself. Focusing on the present displaces worries about the past and the future.

A: negative experience of house before gardening

B: negative experience of house after gardening

Bridge of thought and emotion elides the space (garden) between A and B

Positive experience keeps A and B separate – you enjoy your time in the garden

When taking positive steps to confront a real-life challenge, something similar happens. So long as you are absorbed in your positive response, you are creating something that for the moment usurps your sorrow. When you do find yourself returning to your pain, directing compassion at it will override any tendency towards impatience or anger. Your pain will be there still, but you will not be magnifying it through the distorting lens of negative emotions.

Our ability to evolve through times of darkness and live as our authentic selves, moment by moment, even while experiencing pain, is indomitable if we choose it to be so.

Resilience under
STRAIN

You will probably have seen people who cope brilliantly with the pressures they face. Some show tremendous courage, rising to monumental challenges while even managing to show flashes of humour. Such inner strength is, in fact, available to us all, if only we find the right star by which to navigate through our darkness.

Self-exploration can teach us to separate the true self from its material circumstances. To express the matter in Buddhist terms, the pain we feel when our beloved project collapses or our closest friend is taken from us by a fatal illness is the pain of attachment. This pain can be reduced by an adjustment of our priorities. By looking with detachment through our emotional blizzard to perceive what really matters to us, and using those priorities as orientation points to steer by, we can negotiate the best possible route through adversity. As the German philosopher Friedrich Nietzsche put it, "He who has a why to live can bear almost any how."

Finding detachment need not be in any way selfish, although we might initially feel guilty even at the idea of removing ourselves from the pain of loss. The truth is actually the converse of this: the ego is more involved in hanging on than in letting go.

Finding a way

The most valuable orientation points for deeply troubling experiences are probably going to be love, compassion and spirit. Your faith may not involve belief in a deity or even be expressible as a set of firm convictions, but that doesn't relegate the concept to irrelevance. If you are a humanist, you will have faith in living well without thought of reward, even in the hereafter. You might still, as an atheist, have faith in spirit. But the advantage of choosing love as your compass bearing is that it cuts through all theological and spiritual complexities as a universal affirmation of value. If you feel the need for a star to guide your steps, nothing shines brighter or longer.

Remember, too, that you will not find a *cure* for the pain you are enduring. In your journey of self-development, a change in consciousness will be more precious and more real than any supposed solution.

Shrink the
PAIN DRAGON

Physical pain is something that can test your resilience to the limits. This practice offers a way to manage the pain by using the experience itself as the focus of a meditation.

ATTEND TO YOUR PAIN

Describe the pain to yourself in detail. Where is it located? Is it moving around or does it sit statically in one place? Is it sharp or dull? Is it throbbing? What is the impact of the pain on your surrounding muscles?

FORM AN IMAGE

Visualize your pain as a sac of plasma sitting in your body. Give it a colour that seems suitable to you – perhaps red for intensity, or blue if it seems like a turbulent inner sea. Focus your mind wholly on your pain, altering the image to suit any changes in the pain experience.

BREATHE YOUR PAIN SMALLER

Breathe slowly and deeply. As you breathe out, visualize the pain sac getting smaller as some of its contents leave your body. When you breathe in again, bring the pain back. What you are doing is learning to control the pain. Each time you bring it back to yourself, see it as slightly smaller. In a series of gradual steps, you move towards greater ease. In due course the pain will be noticeably diminished.

Healthy
BOUNDARIES

Putting up metaphorical boundaries is an essential coping strategy, serving two main purposes. It helps us to keep pressure at bay, and it enables us to create spaces where we can take a break from our challenges to do something we enjoy, as refreshment for the tired spirit.

The idea of consciously building walls in our lives might seem out of tune with the mind–body–spirit ethos, which prefers to emphasize unity and openness. We are unlikely these days to believe in a firm division between the mind and the body. And letting others into our lives rather than excluding them is certainly a foundation stone of inner tranquillity.

However, there are certain boundaries we can create in our lives to help us through tough times. This is nothing to do with closing off our hearts, only of closing off our time. It's a matter partly of separating ourselves from potential overload, and partly of creating protected places of retreat for self-nurture.

The power of "no"

When we are having a tough time, that does not immunize us against the possibility of further problems being piled on our plates. Some of these we just have to deal with, on top of everything else – life is just like that sometimes. However, you might well decide to exercise your right of refusal in such situations: to raise a wall to protect yourself.

The classic example is being asked to take on a task or errand that under ordinary circumstances you would accept. By saying "no" this time, you conserve your time and inner resources to deal with more urgent matters. Of course, if you feel a distraction would be beneficial, you could choose to accept this new commission. But politely putting up a boundary would be a valid option and one that might prevent you from overstretching yourself. Saying "yes" when your intuition urges you to say "no" could be something you could come to regret.

Bear in mind the following if you feel guilty about denying a request from someone you like:

- Saying "yes" but being unable in the end to follow through on the commitment would be unfair to this person.
- Agreeing to do this might compromise your existing commitments to others, which are difficult already given the challenges you face.

"In dealing with those who are undergoing great suffering, if you feel 'burnout' setting in, if you feel demoralized and exhausted, it is best, for the sake of everyone, to withdraw and restore yourself."

HIS HOLINESS THE 14TH DALAI LAMA

➲ Saying "yes" might make it impossible for you to deal with more important situations that may later arise.

Finally, saying "yes" when deep in your heart you know you should have said "no" can undermine your self-esteem – your view of yourself as acting as proficiently and effectively as you can in difficult circumstances.

A space for the self

The classic example of needing to create a walled-off space for regular self-nurture occurs with people who are responsible, at least in part, for the care of family members. Caregiving generates strain over extended periods, comes with high levels of unpredictable and uncontrollable behaviour, and often sends secondary stress rippling into other areas of life. There may also be a sense of hopelessness in knowing your loved one will never get better. In such a situation, taking regular breaks for rest, variety, keeping fit and doing your usual self-development practice – and, whenever possible, for keeping up connections in your social circle – is vital.

In fact, whatever the particular character of your challenge, there can be no better tonic than doing something positive and enjoyable for yourself. Set up a boundary, perhaps seeing this as a wall around yourself, and treat it as sacrosanct. Admit into this space only people who make you feel good – people you love to spend time with.

Talking and
SHARING

There's no merit to be gleaned from absorbing all your problems, without letting anyone else have a glimpse of what you are going through. You owe it to yourself and your loved ones to seek help whenever you are attempting to weather tough times.

When we try to put a lid on our problems, they tend to get bigger. If we can find the right person to talk to, it can help us to see our own fears more clearly and perhaps obtain valuable feedback. Chatting to someone who has been through similar experiences can make you feel less alone, less singled out by fate.

In selecting someone to share with, identify in advance what you are looking for. Consider the following options, depending on the variety of support you are seeking:

● **QUIET, PATIENT LISTENER** This kind of person is ideal when you just want to talk. Encouraging them to ask questions can help you gain clarity. Choose someone empathic. It might be an idea to prepare them for the possibility of tears – ensure it's someone to whom you can show emotions without being embarrassed.

● **CLEAR, RATIONAL THINKER** Such a listener might be helpful if you think you are the victim of your own muddled thinking and would like someone to shine the torch of reason for you. Ask yourself, however, if they might become frustrated by your own more intuitive or emotional approach. It would be unwise to choose someone who might be dismissive.

● **EFFECTIVE, ARTICULATE PRAGMATIST** A supporter who can imaginatively enter the world of your problems and help you find solutions can be invaluable, but this is asking a lot of them, so it needs to be someone you know really well.

● **COMMITTED, SUPPORTIVE CHAMPION** Sometimes you might need someone to speak on your behalf – to act as a kind of ambassador. Try to think of someone who is confident and persuasive. In certain conflict situations, you might like to bring your pragmatist friend with you, as a witness to difficult encounters.

● **GENTLE, CARING CONSOLER** This is someone who understands that just being there, and being hugged or touched affectionately, is all you need. Words are unnecessary. The love that flows from touch is deeply healing.

The giving impulse

Many people in difficulty are reluctant to draw attention to their plight, believing that even telling their story may feel like an imposition. Against this, you need to consider the importance many people attach to useful service. Going out of your way to be helpful is a norm of friendship, and you need have no in-principle reason not to ask friends for their support. They will often be more than happy to give it.

Calling upon family may sometimes be less appropriate. They might be too bound up in your situation and unable to provide the detachment a friend can often bring. On the other hand, a sibling relationship, in particular, will often be a source of strength.

"Be an opener of doors for such as come after thee and do not try to make the universe a blind alley."

RALPH WALDO EMERSON (1803–1882)

Outside the circle

Deep stress can lead to poor health, as we have seen, and so to call upon professional healing expertise is often the wisest course of action. Complementary therapies such as herbal remedies and flower essences may also be of help.

Online forums can be a wonderful way of sharing, and of learning from others' experiences, though try not to make this your only source of guidance, as this can lead to lonely, worried hours in front of a screen. There's no substitute for real contact with really helpful people.

In extreme situations you might like to talk to someone working for an appropriate charity, such as Samaritans. It's worth doing some online research to find out what help is available. Regardless of your faith, there may also be religious networks that can help. See what's out there, and contact the organizations you feel most comfortable with for support.

"Do what you can, with what you have, where you are."

THEODORE ROOSEVELT (1858–1919)

Welcoming the
POSITIVE

In tough times you are almost certainly going to want to try more than one method of coping. The best policy is to prepare and strengthen yourself on a whole range of fronts simultaneously if you can. By ensuring you are still pursuing positive experiences, you can give your life the best chance of retaining something like its previous sense of balance.

When facing serious challenges, you will need to ensure you are benefiting from whatever sources of well-being are available to you; otherwise, the challenges may draw you in and come to dominate your whole inner landscape. A road map of key dimensions of well-being is shown below and overleaf. When engaging in these areas, positive things are likely to happen – experiences in which you can take satisfaction or pleasure. Relish them

THE ROAD MAP FOR BALANCE
Here is an overview of the areas to which attention should be given if you seek to maintain healing balance in your life during troubled times.

TAKE TIME OUT from the daily struggle. If you attend an evening class, keep your lessons sacrosanct. If you love music, make an effort to take in a concert. Find time to read and make space for silence.

EAT AND SLEEP WELL Take regular, healthy meals. Cultivate good sleep routines. Avoid too much alcohol.

EXERCISE DAILY Sharing exercise with a friend occasionally gives you the chance to socialize, while keeping yourself in trim.

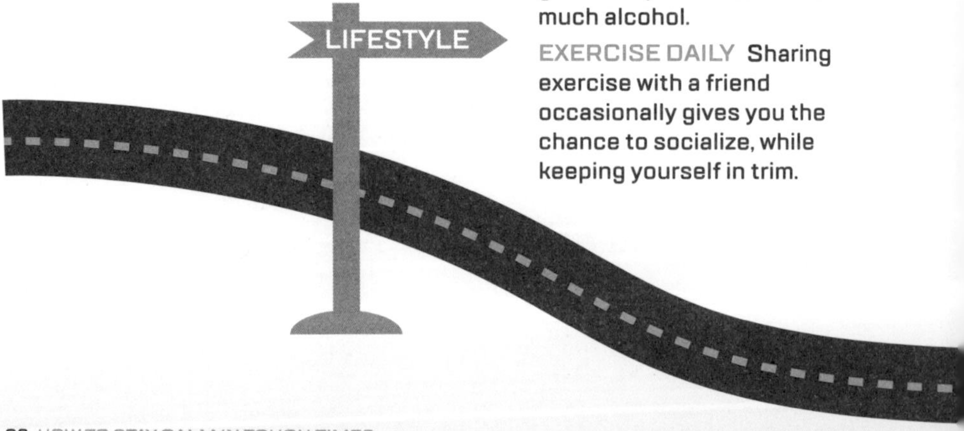

LIFESTYLE

> "Be moderate in order to taste the joys of life in abundance."
>
> EPICURUS (341–270 BCE)

whenever they occur. The same applies, of course, to positive outcomes in the course of dealing with your challenges – moments of achievement, humour, relief, insight, strength, reward and so on are all worthy of celebration.

The time issue

When you have lots of problems to solve, or one or two big problems, or when you feel otherwise under pressure, you will often find it necessary to cut back some of your discretionary activities. If this is the case, look at the road map carefully and ring-fence the ones you feel are indispensable. All the "lifestyle" points are essential and not inordinately time-consuming if you cut back your social activities to, say, a weekly or at least fortnightly treat. You may feel the need to cut down on community involvement (many people make this sacrifice with some relief), but do keep your network alive as much

BODY WORK Yoga, Pilates or Tai Chi all help to make you feel more comfortable in your skin, with a reasonable mind–body–spirit balance.

RELAXATION If nothing else, do simple breathing exercises daily. Use them at times of stress to calm your emotions and gain a clearer mental perspective.

MEDITATION Meditate at least weekly. Mindfulness meditation is a good starting point, but other options include mantra meditation and TCM (transcendental meditation).

CONNECTION

PRACTICE

SOCIAL Keeping up your friendships gives you a source of refreshment and support, as well as a framework for positive activities such as sport, leisure trips and cultural outings.

LOVE provides a healing ambience and a lodestone of value. Ensure that amid your talk about problems you also find time for intimacy, shared appreciation of life's blessings and celebration.

continued over

COMMUNITY Involvement in the local community, in the form of giving (service, money or support), enlarges your horizons and enables you to feel that you matter.

as possible, through the occasional phone call, email or meeting. The ideal solution is to ration the social activities on the checklist, if necessary, rather than drop them – all the other items are vital.

Trying to live simply – for example, by making social arrangements that are easy to set up – can help you to economize on time spent. If it helps, let your friends handle the logistics. On a question of lifestyle, a healthy meal can be quicker and easier to prepare than a self-indulgent one.

"It is better to rise from life as from a banquet – neither thirsty nor drunken."

ARISTOTLE (384–322 BCE)

LEARNING Be aware of what you are discovering about yourself in the way you react or respond to every challenge. Attend to your emotions with as much detachment as you can muster. Learn your capabilities as they unfold.

ATTITUDES Monitor your assumptions in a questioning spirit. Consider the impact of your attitudes on the way you tackle your challenges and on their outcomes.

CHANGES Identify and work on any changes you can make to your mindset to find more fulfilment and less stress in your life (see pages 50–59).

PROBLEM SOLVING

INNER GROWTH

ANALYSIS Facing up to your problems and examining their strands individually will bring you, ultimately, more peace of mind than strategies of evasion.

CHOICES Set aside quiet periods when you can reflect on the available choices for working through your issues. Then select the options that seem most promising and test them against your intuition.

ACTION Put your choices into effect, one by one, following a predetermined schedule. Use time-management techniques to keep pressure at bay. Build into your schedule plenty of other points from this road map to give you breaks and avoid pushing yourself too hard.

Dealing with
LOSS

Before we take our own leave of this life, we will encounter mortality as loss. Whether or not we saw it coming, the impact will be deep, and there are no quick fixes to lessen the pain. All we can do is accept our emotions, live our own grieving, look after ourselves and resume a full life when we are ready.

It's common to feel a mixture of emotions after losing someone close to you. There's no uniform way to experience loss or to grieve. Alongside sadness, shock and despair, the more surprising feelings of guilt, anger and relief often surface from time to time, and it's important you do not feel at any time that your response is inappropriate or strange – it isn't.

Family tensions can often arise between people who are coping with bereavement in different ways – for example, one wanting to talk, the other preferring quiet solitude. Look out for such stresses, and be as tolerant as you can of different coping styles.

Shock can be felt even by those who believe they are well prepared. Many people cry every day for a while and may be angry with themselves for their lack of self-control. You may feel you just cannot cope with such strong feelings. Although this may sound like empty words, the feelings *will* eventually become less intense and you will find a way to live with them.

The strong yearning we often feel for the one we have lost is particularly difficult to cope with. We may feel desperate to *find* them, despite the impossibility of this. Such feelings can make it extremely hard to relax or to concentrate on anything else.

Self-care

Loss commonly brings physical symptoms, too, including insomnia, appetite loss (or overeating) and headaches. Looking after your body as well as possible, by making the right choices about diet and exercise, is of the utmost importance.

The phrase "Take it one day at a time", so often said, has real value as an inner mantra that you can repeat to ensure you narrow your horizons of anxiety. Worrying about tomorrow's problems now is unhelpful: better to focus in a practical way on what you have to get through today.

Keeping busy is one way of coping; but an equally helpful approach for many is to take things slowly and perhaps book a holiday or go for long walks. Being among other people can feel reassuring, even if you don't yet feel ready to engage with anyone.

Anniversaries

For most of us, seeing the body comes early in the grieving process, whether before or after the undertaker has been summoned. This is distressing but offers an emotionally constructive way to say "goodbye". Not doing this, or not giving a tribute at the funeral, can give rise to deep regret later.

Generally, we find it valuable to commemorate those we have lost. An annual visit to their grave or the place where their ashes lie is a way to ritually affirm their importance. Some of us will opt to visit more often. Planting a tree, which grows taller as time advances, can have a suggestive symbolism, with overtones of new growth as well as memory.

In time, such ritual actions, especially if they take place in lovely surroundings, can induce a sense of peace, based on loving memories and continuing connection. Devise any ritual that seems intuitively right for you – it could be a regular pilgrimage to a holiday destination. The seaside and mountains, in particular, offer a symbolic resonance that seems to help healing and promote acceptance and tranquillity.

When to seek help

Talking with family and friends can be a great source of comfort. Some might go further and seek the help of a bereavement counsellor, even a year or more after the person passed away. Any of the following effects should prompt you to consider this option if they continue to happen long after the event:

- ➡ Feeling unable to get up and face the day.
- ➡ Complete loss of appetite, or other aspects of physical self-neglect.
- ➡ Seeing your life ahead as unbearable.
- ➡ Emotions so intense they undermine normal life.

If you are struggling with your feelings, even before you lose someone, a bereavement counsellor will be able to help you.

"He who has gone, so we but cherish his memory, abides with us, more potent, nay, more present than the living man."

ANTOINE DE SAINT-EXUPÉRY (1900–1944)

WHAT TO EXPECT IN LOSS

Individuals differ greatly in the way they experience and show grief, and rigid generalizations are unhelpful. However, most people seem to recover from a major bereavement after a couple of years. The following symptoms are likely to occur, following each other or overlapping in unpredictable ways.

⊙ SHOCK This occurs even if the death was expected. Numbness, a common manifestation, can be helpful when you are dealing with the practical arrangements following a loss.

⊙ AGITATION The emotional turbulence immediately after the passing tends to reach a peak about two weeks later.

⊙ SADNESS Periods of sadness or depression increase in frequency after the time of agitation. They often peak after four to six weeks.

⊙ STRONG GRIEF Grief can break out in spasms at any time, usually in response to some cue that has triggered a reminder of the person.

⊙ ANGER You may feel angry at the fate that has taken away a loved one, or at the person themselves for making you lonely and upset. You may also feel anger about people who don't understand the depth of your loss.

⊙ GUILT It's common to feel guilty about things said or done, or neglected. You might even, irrationally, feel guilt about the death itself, as if you could have prevented it or made it less painful.

⊙ RESUMPTION It's usually good to try to resume something that resembles normal life after about two weeks. It might be tempting even after that to avoid seeing people who strike you as indifferent or unempathic, but doing so can cause complications.

⊙ REFLECTION Quiet reflection on the lost person and the times you shared is an essential part of grieving. To outsiders it can seem that you are lost in your own world.

Coping with
ILLNESS

Illness can transform the way we see ourselves and the possibilities available to us. Whether we are the patient, or involved in caring for someone close to us, we need to focus on the positive without pushing away the true facts of the situation. Denial is as damaging to our peace as deep pessimism.

People who are sick cannot be expected to feel positive all the time. Pressure from family or friends to look on the bright side isn't helpful. Psychologists say that those battling against illness want others to acknowledge how tough it is for them. The best approach is to let sick people experience their bad emotions. More positive feelings, and more effective coping, may then follow.

Creating the right balance between hopelessness and false cheeriness is tricky, and some false steps are to be expected. Cautious optimism, combined with an acceptance of the facts, is the optimum approach.

It's helpful when you are ill to concentrate on what you can control. The key factors will be diet, exercise and decisions that need making about doctors and treatment. Having sympathetic family and friends around you, who will listen patiently as you describe all manner of emotions, is also a great benefit.

The journey from diagnosis

As you get to know your illness and learn how to manage it, the initial shock or fear may shade into:

➔ **ANGER** Why have I been chosen to have this problem?
➔ **SADNESS** How can I be happy now that I can't live as before?
➔ **CONFUSION** How will I look after myself?

Many coming to terms with serious illness say they no longer feel like a whole person. Shame and embarrassment may come into the mix. Such emotions need to be acknowledged and reflected on. In time, whatever limitations you have to accept, such as self-injection or regular hospital visits, will become a new normal. Give yourself time to learn about your illness. During the learning process you will almost inevitably encounter stress (see pages 12–31). Therapy sessions can be helpful if the stress lasts or is intense.

Many people find it helpful to talk straightforwardly about their illness, naming it rather than using euphemisms to protect the sensibilities of the listener. Once you have started doing this, and finding that people have no problems with frank talk, it soon becomes a natural part of your mindset.

HOW TO BE A CALM CARER

Being a carer for a loved one, though demanding, can also bring something valuable into your relationship. The key to success is balancing your own needs with those of your dependant. Here are some guidelines for success.

- ➔ **INVOLVE** the person in decision-making as much as possible.
- ➔ **PROVIDE** plenty of stimulus – plan get-togethers with friends and try to organize nice surprises.
- ➔ **LOOK AFTER** your own health through good diet and plenty of exercise.
- ➔ **EXPRESS LOVE** in your body language and words.
- ➔ **BE WATCHFUL** – you might welcome silence, but could it indicate a problem?
- ➔ **SEE YOUR CARE** as a deserved flow from your compassionate heart.
- ➔ **ENJOY MINDFULNESS** practice with the person if they have dementia, since focusing on the moment makes good sense if memory is seriously defective.
- ➔ **LOOK FOR HAPPINESS,** not suffering – moments of joy will only come if you are open to them.
- ➔ **AVOID ROLE STEREOTYPES,** such as the carer as endlessly energetic, and the dependant as lacking will or interests.

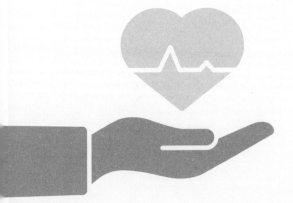

"He who takes medicine and neglects to diet wastes the skill of his doctors."

CHINESE PROVERB

THOUGHT PLAN

Making
CALM SPACES

3 AFFIRMATIONS

➔ "I'm learning to find peace in the good spaces between challenging moments."

➔ "I'm steering the best possible course through the storm with the support of my wonderful friends."

➔ "I'm staying true to my values, and with their help I'm staying true to my essential self, whatever happens."

7 THOUGHT POINTS

➔ Avoid future-storms

A "future-storm" happens when all the hypothetical problems and outcomes that concern you about the future rush into your mind and fill it with panic. This derives mostly from low self-esteem in difficult times. Remember that a possibility is not automatically a probability. Try to detect the "knowing my luck" syndrome in your thinking – for example, "knowing my luck, the new high-speed railway will come within a mile of my home, making it impossible to sell". Bad luck happens but is not self-perpetuating.

➔ Treat work worries as service

We spend a great deal of our lives at work, often dealing with problems that are not personal. If worrying is what you are paid to do, try to remember that this is the case whenever work worries threaten to coalesce into other difficulties, making it tough to find peace. Switch off your work mode when you head home at the day's end – you are not paid to take work worries home with you.

● Feel emotions fully

Many people, anxious that their emotions have the potential to be overwhelming, put up an inner barrier around them to diminish their impact. They think about them, replaying events in their mind, but hold back from fully *feeling* them. If you allow yourself to experience loss, pain, sadness or anger authentically, you are less likely to be trapped in these feelings for such long periods. Accepting the full force of emotion makes it easier to move on.

● Know your terrain

When bad luck happens, it's often tempting to think of life as a lottery that just isn't going your way and where the fates have conspired against you. In fact, it's more productive to think of luck as the environment in which life operates. There will be outcomes of all kinds, some of which are preferable to others. But life's whole mission is to find the best fulfilment you can, steering by the best values, within this environment.

● See past the hardship

Draw upon previous experience, if you can, to see beyond your current difficulties to the time when they will be behind you. If you are experiencing panic, for example, you know from your personal history that such feelings subside quite quickly. If your son is going through an aggressive phase, you know from parenting his older brother that this will pass in time. Meanwhile, all you can do is your best.

● Apply the money test

It used to be said, as an item of proverbial wisdom, that if a problem can be fixed by money, it's not really a problem. The deepest problems, according to this view, are immune to monetary solutions. It's worth applying this measure early on in your assessment of the level of challenge you face. If your particular problems are of the kind that cash cannot solve, it's still good to put them into perspective.

● Keep a true sense of self

When struggling against serious difficulties, we often start to define ourselves in terms of our challenges, as if they have become an aspect of our character. This is unfortunate for a number of reasons. It tends to make resolving our problems more difficult, it undervalues our potential and our abilities, chipping away at our self-esteem, and it makes it harder for us to find inner peace. Know that your true self, with all the values you steer by, remains intact whatever challenges are thrown your way.

ACTION PLAN

Weathering THE STORM

10 ACTION POINTS

➔ Work around selfishness

Many of the people we have to deal with are very different from ourselves in temperament and values. From time to time you will come across someone so selfish, thoughtless or illogical that you find them astonishing. Don't waste time and energy wondering how they can possibly behave as they do. Accept that these people have failings, and don't do them the honour of spending any of your emotional energy on them. Just find workarounds to overcome the barriers they pose.

➔ Make the most of interruptions

Imagine that you are battling emotionally and on a practical level in a messy divorce. A friend is holding a big party to celebrate winning a prize. You are so bogged down in your troubles that you dread this distraction, though you feel you have to attend. In such circumstances, see what happens if you do a mental flip that turns dread to welcome. Sharing in a celebration is exactly the kind of pleasant counterpoint that will lift your spirits in tough times. Look forward to the break, put your troubles on hold and enjoy the occasion mindfully.

➔ Find peace in music

Music can offer surprisingly deep sources of peace in troubled times. Even if you love music that's vibrant and exciting, put your preferences aside and explore quieter music, too. Classical pieces that stand out for their peacefulness include Debussy, *Clair de Lune*; Satie, *Trois Gymnopédies*; Handel, *Water Music*; Bach, *Air on the G String*. There is also ambient music, including a wealth of mind–body–spirit sounds composed specifically for relaxation.

➔ Solve it by walking

Solvitur ambulando ("solve it by walking") is a Latin motto everyone should take to heart. Going for a walk, whether in peaceful surroundings or just around a city block, gives us time for healing reflection as well as the benefits of gentle exercise. The rhythm of footsteps may also be subliminally relaxing.

➡ Ask for what you need

When drawing upon support from friends or family, be as clear as you can about your particular needs. For example, you might just want a shoulder to cry on, rather than practical advice of a kind you feel is unsuitable for your situation. Or you might want some moral support, rather than hearing about someone who could be blamed for your problems when you have specifically chosen not to focus on blame. Set clear boundaries so the help you do *not* want gets filtered out.

➡ Terminate a crisis

We often feel ourselves to be still in crisis long after the true crisis has passed. For example, during a relationship break-up you may have moved beyond decision-making to dealing with the aftermath – the practicalities of who lives where and so on. In such circumstances, it can be helpful to declare the crisis over. There may still be issues ahead, but it's harmful to think you are in crisis when in fact you are well into the recovery stage.

➡ Prioritize essential needs

Your empathy may make you feel for someone affected by your actions. There will be times, though, when you have to put your own needs first. Imagine that you and a friend are in business together and you find the responsibilities so stressful you have decided to end your involvement. You know your friend will be devastated by your decision, so show compassion in conveying the news, but don't let your sympathy hold you back from following your intuition.

➡ Say what you believe

When under any kind of pressure, you may feel that pressure will only increase if you express opinions that go against everyone's expectations. However, sometimes it's necessary to risk unpopularity. Some people, in any case, might admire you for speaking your mind. By not saying something you believe to be true, you could be storing up trouble for yourself down the line.

➡ Immerse yourself in nature

The natural world offers a healing perspective on our difficulties. Even in an urban environment, there will be something natural to appreciate – from exotic trees in the park to a peregrine nesting on a cathedral tower. Take binoculars out with you. See what you can see. Mindful absorption in nature, even briefly, is subtly calming.

➡ Just do something

At times of confusion or uncertainty, when you feel trapped by troubles, just do something – make a to-do list, call someone or do some internet research. It feels empowering to take action, even on a modest scale. You have moved one step forwards, so appreciate your decisiveness and keep up the good work.

How to be happy
WITH WHAT
YOU HAVE

The Buddhist idea of nonattachment is now
commonplace in mind–body–spirit thinking, and many
try to follow this basic precept without being wholly
successful. The concept applies to material things, our
ego's desires, our emotions and the people in our lives.
One version of happiness rolls all these components into
a single blissful vision: a successful marriage, well-aligned
and high-achieving children, a large comfortable house
with a garden, a well-rewarded, high-status job.

CHAPTER 5

"What a wonderful life I've had!
I only wish I'd realized it sooner."

COLETTE (1873–1954)

What's wrong with having this as a goal? Nothing, so long
as you don't pin your hopes of happiness exclusively
on the attainment of that goal. True happiness is not
contingent upon any kind of attainment, except that of
being authentic to the self, prioritizing worthwhile values
and leading a life of love, generosity and acceptance,
while focusing on the present moment. Happiness
comes from the riches you already have within yourself,
and self-discovery can lead you straight to them.

Understanding
TRUE WEALTH

Our true wealth lies within ourselves and in our relationships with others. This means that, even if we are unlucky in pursuing our ambitions, we have certain constants in our lives, to serve as a firm basis of contentment.

The things we regard as essential in our lives are defined by our values. In this area of thinking there will be certain red lines we always refuse to cross. Most would be unwilling to steal, defraud or blackmail, with honesty trumping self-interest. Truth is more complicated: for example, we might lie to protect others from pain. Our values are not automatic reflexes; we choose them carefully, taking into account the complexities of real life.

Every individual is different, but the following could be regarded as core necessities, in which our true wealth lies:

- **AUTHENTICITY** Being true to our perception of who we are. We are inauthentic if we say one thing and mean another – that is insincerity.
- **LOVE** Without love in our lives, our experiences are narrow and unrewarding. Allied to this is compassion.
- **CONNECTION** This is manifested in our communications with others, including the professional helpers in our lives. Without connection we usually feel isolated.
- **EXPRESSION** We need to express our emotions to those close to us, or we are likely to be overwhelmed by them.
- **TRUTH** This is related to authenticity, but the specific aspect intended here is the avoidance of selfish deceit.
- **SELFLESSNESS** To follow selfish aims is to ruthlessly turn our back on others. Giving and self-sacrifice are the ultimate expressions of this.
- **TALENTS** Everyone has some kind of talent. The spectrum ranges from being thoughtful and empathic with people, to the specialized skills we have learned for work. Creativity falls within this category.

Perhaps our true wealth lies in this collection of qualities, or something like it. To these items you might be tempted to add health, fitness and comfort, but the problem of letting happiness rest on these factors is that they cannot be taken for granted. For this reason, we should be grateful if we have them; but if we don't, happiness is not denied us.

The happiness quest

Happiness is notoriously hard to assess, and the process of trying to do so may be perversely stressful. When we measure ourselves against our visionary yardstick, how should we feel when we fall short? Frustrated, perhaps.

The truth is that worrying too much about happiness can obscure our understanding of what already gives us contentment in our lives. To live mindfully, with good intentions and with love, accepting what is beyond our control, learning to be the person we choose to be and dealing with any challenges as they arise, is a formula for happiness that cannot be improved.

"Most folks are about as happy as they make up their minds to be."

ABRAHAM LINCOLN (1809–1865)

HIDDEN STREAMS

It's likely that happiness already runs in different threads through our life without our sufficiently noticing it. To correct this defect of perception, and wake to a new, grateful awareness of your deepest wealth, ask yourself whether happiness might lie in any of the following:

- Being the person we are when our feelings, thoughts, behaviour and speech are all consistent with each other and with our values.

- Living without regret for the past or fear of the future.

- A deep sense of being at ease with life that underlies all emotions, including sadness.

- The experience of perceiving beauty all around us, including in people's hearts.

Self-knowledge and
SELF-ACCEPTANCE

Self-knowledge means looking at all aspects of ourselves with the minimum of positive or negative bias. Self-acceptance means warmly accepting the seeking, learning self as it tries to live by its values and make the most of its strengths.

Understanding emotions leads us to grasp why we do what we do, which makes up our habits. And realizing the reasons for our habits makes it easier for us to change them if they are not serving our needs satisfactorily.

Paradoxically, while moving towards such changes, we all benefit from accepting ourselves as learning, developing people. There will be areas where further advances are needed. However, we would do well to accept the self, at a fundamental level, rather than always feeling that we are inadequate.

There's no contradiction in the idea that we can accept our essential selves without leaving the habits that undermine our well-being as they are. It's easy to get into a conceptual tangle here. If our experiences shape us, does that mean that the self is partly composed of those experiences? The answer has to be "no", or else an abusive partner, for example, could transform us into a victim. We may feel like a victim, long after, but then decide, if we are strong, that the feeling is based on an error of self-perception. The self is the agency making that decision about how to respond to an aspect of its past experience.

Self-acceptance means forgiving ourselves for our reactions to all that has happened to us. We may have done something really unkind once, which may have sprung from insecurity or some other psychic scar. If we learned a lesson, there's no point holding on to toxic regret or self-blame. The self is constantly creating a new present, one where we can grow out of our limitations.

The personality question

Whereas, in the past, psychologists spoke of personality as a spectrum of "types", it's more common now to find references to personality *tendencies*. Carl Jung, who coined the terms "introvert" and "extravert", saw these as an absolute pairing: you could be either one or the other. These days it's generally believed that most people are a mix of the two, with a tendency in one direction.

Our personality tendencies are not necessarily permanent, if we can identify them and adopt new habits that start to undermine the old patterns. Even the social roles we take on can shape us. First-time parents or those with new jobs may find their new responsibilities push them to alter how they think, feel and behave. As we age, we tend to become more conscientious and agreeable and more emotionally stable. As our lives develop, so do our personalities.

Personality
PENTANGLE

Psychologists often score people in terms of the Big Five personality traits. These are listed here, not with the sometimes negative labels applied to high or low scores, but with more positive adjectives. Use these words as the basis for a self-review, writing down for each of the five traits two aspects that seem to fit you. Which of these tendencies do you want to encourage and which do you wish to try to adjust?

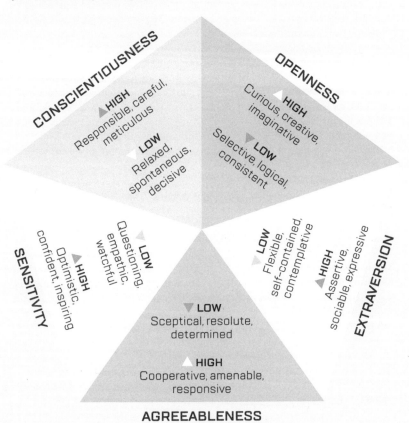

CONSCIENTIOUSNESS

▲ **HIGH** Responsible, careful, meticulous

▼ **LOW** Relaxed, spontaneous, decisive

OPENNESS

▲ **HIGH** Curious, creative, imaginative

▼ **LOW** Selective logical, consistent

SENSITIVITY

▲ **HIGH** Optimistic, confident, inspiring

▲ **LOW** Questioning, empathic, watchful

EXTRAVERSION

▲ **LOW** Flexible, self-contained, contemplative

▲ **HIGH** Assertive, sociable, expressive

AGREEABLENESS

▼ **LOW** Sceptical, resolute, determined

△ **HIGH** Cooperative, amenable, responsive

Overcoming
DISAPPOINTMENT

Disappointment arises from the dashing of our hopes. We must be careful how we respond when the emotion hits us, or we can find ourselves caught up in negative thinking that serves us ill by blinding us to what is good in our lives, including our future possibilities.

Disappointment comes in different strengths, and taking too narrow a view of your situation, and the options available to you, tends to increase the perceived intensity. One way of taking some of the sting away might be for you to imagine an event in the context of a whole chapter of your life – perhaps the year you are living through, or even two or more years. That might lessen the impact. Whatever happened might, of course, be a serious blow to your plans or hopes, and not all disappointments can be scaled down by looking at the bigger picture. But it's certainly worth trying this approach.

If you can diminish the impact of a disappointment, by seeing it in its true perspective, you reduce the possibility it will turn into irritation, anger, resentment, bitterness or jealousy. If you allow it to morph into a stronger emotion, such as depression or discouragement, you may start to let the negatives in your life overshadow the positives, missing the opportunities to realize your full potential. Coming to terms with disappointment in a timely fashion, while allowing it time to settle in your mind first, is the wisest approach.

A five-step strategy
Psychologists recommend the following procedure to deal with disappointment and the options you will probably need to consider after experiencing it:

1 ACKNOWLEDGE THE EMOTION
Some disappointments are straightforward – you have failed an exam, say, or lost the buyer for an apartment you need to sell. Sometimes, however, there are other emotions mingled in. For example, if you are disappointed not to be invited to a party, there may be an element of jealousy. Spend a little time recognizing your feelings and assessing their strength. Don't make any decisions or take any action until they have settled down.

2 DISENTANGLE YOURSELF
Don't take disappointment too personally. If you have low self-esteem, you might well attribute the outcome of an event to your own failings, whereas in fact those failings stem from complexities of cause and effect in the life

around you. If someone else got a job you wanted, that's an event in *their* life, not yours. You aren't to blame for the outcome.

3 ASSESS YOUR EXPECTATIONS

This is a good time to ask whether your expectations suit your purpose. It's possible they were inappropriate or unrealistic. Consider whether you need to adjust them now to match the outcome or what it has taught you about yourself.

4 ZOOM OUT

Having focused on the event, zoom out to take a broad look at the whole context. What can you learn from the experience? Maybe, despite the disappointment, there are good things to take into account: better opportunities, a better way forwards. Self-reflection after disappointment is often productive.

5 TRY AGAIN – OR CHANGE YOUR INTENTION

Don't automatically assume that trying again will lead to just another failure. It may be worth trying a new way of approaching such challenges. On the other hand, there may be something in the situation that means your second attempt will bring the same result. Your self-reflection, if you have followed these steps, should have cast some light on this. Finding a new goal, but without any bitterness over perceived failure, might be the best plan – in which case, the disappointment has yielded a positive result.

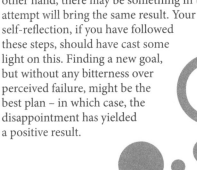

"There are some defeats more triumphant than victories."

MICHEL DE MONTAIGNE (1533–1592)

Managing
YOUR ROLES

Our roles are socially determined. The responsibilities of one role will often clash with those of another. When we demand too much of ourselves, these conflicts are capable of being stressful. But if we can manage our roles with pragmatic acceptance of our inability to reach perfection, we have the potential to derive greater satisfaction from them.

It's difficult for any of us to give a simple answer to the self-addressed question "Who am I?" In attempting a response, our thoughts may flit over our roles in life, the self we would like to be (perhaps occupying more suitable roles) and the public image we present to others. This image may be at odds – even quite radically so – with our self-perception. For example, it might involve giving people the impression that we are occupying a role – mother or son, carer or teacher – more successfully than we feel deep down to be the case. Such a mismatch between inner and outer can be a source of conflict, distracting us from the enjoyments and opportunities that a role potentially offers.

Roles in conflict
Nobody fills a role perfectly. Perfection is an unhelpful ideal to measure yourself by, as you will inevitably fall short. Total success is often compromised by your having at least one other role to fill, in which case tension is almost inevitable. Time and energy are limited, so you must balance priorities, aiming for adequacy rather than supreme achievement in one or all of the roles. Perfectionism, in any case, can be unhealthy, leading to disappointment when a less severe eye would see plenty for you to be happy about.

The life–work balance is the classic area in which compromise must often be accepted. Tension occurs notably between family responsibilities and the money required to fulfil them – though sometimes work is also seen as a source of personal satisfaction, or at least an escape from the home. When juggling like this, one refreshing and energizing thing you can do is make space for the self to recuperate – through downtime or "me time". This gives you a space in which you are free from self-judgment.

A broader strategy, related to "me time", is to keep a clear sense of the essential you. When you define your identity by a role, this limits the scope of your fulfilment to those opportunities the role makes available.

Usually these are limited. There's only so much satisfaction that managers can derive from their careers. A mother's fulfilment in her role may seem infinite, but that cannot quite be true if you accept that motherhood is enriched when you allow yourself to be more than a mother. Parenting isn't just a combination of practicalities and love – it's also endless giving from the whole richness of the self.

VALUING YOUR
performance

There are two opposed attitudes to success, or otherwise, in the performance of a role. Consider these two contrasting journeys, and resolve to opt for the one that is more realistic and more fulfilling.

ATTITUDE
"I do the best job I can within the available parameters."

ATTITUDE
"I don't fill my role as well as I should."

THEREFORE
I take time out when I need to.
Leads to > Relaxation

I regard myself as sufficiently capable.
Leads to > Greater confidence and success

THEREFORE
I overextend myself to come nearer to the ideal.
Leads to > Stress

I have a low estimation of myself.
Leads to >
Lack of confidence
> Stress

I'm open with others about the limitations I work under.
Leads to > Authenticity

I project a public face that disguises my inadequacy.
Leads to >
Inauthenticity > Stress

Finding value
IN WORK

Workers who are motivated by finding meaning in their work are happier and more valued – not least because they help to generate a positive atmosphere. A prerequisite of finding meaning in employment is engagement: the willingness to commit with full attention and energy, drawing upon all relevant talents.

Many of us set out with high hopes on a career path that offers a chance of job satisfaction, based on a good match of tasks to talents. Whether we reach our destination is another matter, with much depending on the opportunities that arise, our abilities and other factors, such as our personality and family responsibilities. There may also be large social changes at work, enlarging our prospects or shrinking them, as industries wax and wane.

Decision-making

Since going to work is routine, and since there's often an element of routine in the work itself, it's unsurprising that many of us stay in a job through habit. If you are restless, use this summary of options to help you work out the best course of action for your circumstances:

NEW JOB
Promotion
Sideways move
Voluntary demotion

CHANGED YOU
New skills
New attitude
New routine

ADJUSTMENTS TO SAME JOB
More/less work
Different work
Different environment

SEEK FURTHER INFORMATION
From partner/family and friends
From co-workers, management
From counsellor

When you are dissatisfied at work, change is usually called for, but it need not involve a new position. The process might start with an inner change, whereby you come to a different view of the job you have.

Finding meaning

It helps when work gives a sense of achievement – thereby satisfying a basic psychological need. Meaning might also be found in contact with customers or teammates, in the opportunity to work in an attractive environment (an

PURPOSE revisited

When assessing the purpose of a job, look beyond its narrow function to see how it fits into society as a whole. The following activities are all important, and there is no reason not to take pride in them:

- Employing people
- Contributing to the nation's tax revenue
- Bringing staff together in a common enterprise
- Generating subsidiary revenue – perhaps in the canteen, or in office supplies
- Training staff in new skills and approaches
- Perhaps making a contribution to charity
- Encouraging sociable occasions through formal and informal collective effort

art gallery or landscape garden, say), or in belonging to an organization that thinks highly of its staff and rewards initiative.

To help you get a fix on whether you should stay in your current job, ask yourself what is the best meaning you can draw from it. Is that enough? Bear in mind that meaning emerges when you engage wholeheartedly with a job. If you remain detached, meaning will not manifest itself.

Making changes

Many jobs are not absolutely rigid in practice. Employers are often delighted when staff come to them with changes that will benefit everyone – for example, innovative procedures that will boost efficiency.

Ask yourself if there are changes you can offer to make the work more rewarding. If you feel you are underpaid, think how can you argue the case for a rise – maybe you will have to take on more responsibility. Or if you feel underappreciated, maybe you should explain to your employer how this is a major motivation issue.

If your workstation doesn't feel like a personal space that reflects your identity, would you benefit if it were to become so? Consider personalizing your area as much as company policy permits. Also, look for small opportunities to bring more joy and humour into your work, as this can humanize the most serious of workplaces.

At ease with
YOUR BODY

Our relationship with our own body can be fraught with anxiety. Establishing a healthy relationship with the body involves a balance of treating it with self-respect and behaving as if its particular characteristics were unimportant – as, indeed, they are.

The imagery that stares back at us from the media tends to emphasize good looks or physique. It can be hard to stop ourselves making self-denigrating comparisons with the gods and goddesses of perfume and hairspray, aftershave and boxer shorts. Ordinary bodies, especially unfit ones, may seem inadequate by comparison.

What am I like?

The phrase "body image" denotes our internalized sense of what we look like. This is our subjective appearance: what we *think* we look like. Different from this is our objective appearance: how others see us.

For some people, there's good congruence between subjective and objective. Many, though, entertain an idealized body image, reflecting how they would *like* to look. This self-deception is

"Beauty is not in the face; beauty is a light in the heart."

KHALIL GIBRAN (1883–1931)

helped by our clothes, often hiding shape as well as skin; and the face can be disguised by make-up. It could even be argued that few of us see ourselves as we truly are – even in a mirror. The brain tends to edit face and body to fit its wishful thinking.

Older people often turn their focus to worrying about ageing. In this respect, certain emblematic features, such as wrinkles and grey hair, become sources of discontent.

Body image management

Our view of our own appearance feeds back into our behaviour, which in turn affects how others view us. If you keep your head down and avoid eye contact, people might think you are being anti-social. Taken to extremes, body discomfort makes us avoid certain situations, including intimate ones, where our bodies would be seen.

Here are three key principles that can help us to nurture a healthier relationship with our bodies:

1 EAT HEALTHILY AND EXERCISE

If you are neglecting your body, ask yourself why. You may need to trace things back into the past along a causal chain to find the source of, for example, overeating or lack of physical activity. Then choose to replace any negative habits with positive habits so that neglect is transformed to nurture (see pages 54–9).

2 QUESTION FASHIONABLE NORMS

Body fashions are a social construct without authority. If you are curvy rather than slender, or vice versa, so what? The truth is, the human body and face vary hugely, and this variety should be delightful. Society supplies preconceptions crudely. We all have the power to vote otherwise.

3 SEE THE SELF AS ATTRACTIVE

Most people are attracted to personality as much as, or more than, appearance. Another appealing quality is self-possession. From a sense of being at peace with the whole self comes a radiance of gifts. By contrast, anyone not at ease with themselves radiates anxiety.

Judgments

The hair, being pliable into a style, offers a fun way to change our appearance from time to time – even more so than through fashion. Some people at ease in their own skins will take pleasure in this; others will opt for a serviceable style they never, or rarely, change. We should not judge people for whichever approach they choose to follow.

Nor should we judge anyone whose bodily self-consciousness has led them towards cosmetic surgery. If we are compassionate, we will empathize with the anxiety that has led to this. However, to urge someone to go ahead and change their features, if asked for advice, would not be kind. It's better to quote Khalil Gibran's words, quoted opposite. Similar issues also apply to the question of large tattoos.

At ease with
YOUR MIND

The mind is the crucible of our insights, intentions, memories and discoveries. Reason and analysis belong to only a small segment of its scope. Living happily, with full engagement, involves deploying the miraculous capacity of the mind without worrying about what your particular mind *cannot* do.

Socrates said, "I know I am intelligent, because I know that I know nothing." Accepting the limits of the intellect is not only philosophically sound, it's also a good plan for daily life. Other mental attributes available to us include:

- Emotional intelligence
- Interpersonal skills
- Common sense
- Intuition
- Imagination

Emotional intelligence consists of self-awareness, self-management, social awareness and relationship management – all a world away from IQ. People with strengths in these four areas may still, unfortunately, feel inferiority about their smartness or general knowledge, despite the fact that they are so capable within the social context – the context of employment and relationships.

Smartness and knowledge
The truth about IQ is that it's not equally distributed, which means that having a score lower than someone else is rather like not being tall – it's simply a fact. You could say that everyone has their own type of smartness, and we should bear in mind that our mental characteristics, being unique to ourselves, are valuable for that very uniqueness. These might include quirkiness, nimbleness, observation, thoughtfulness, imagination, patience or originality.

Qualifications
Some people who have no qualms about their intelligence nevertheless have anxieties about their education, which may have left gaps in their general knowledge. Not having gone to university can seem a burden to some. Certain circles do, indeed, attach importance to people having a degree. But then, other circles attach importance to people having a pilot's licence or being able to make elderly patients feel cherished. These are professional realms whose values need have no impact on your life (except as a recipient of others' skills).

The questing
MIND REVIEW

Review yourself in terms of the following criteria
to see whether you could be described as having
a questing mind. If you think you fall short in any aspect,
consider whether you would benefit from making some choices
that qualify you more comprehensively. To have a questing
mind, you should:

⟫ LEARN FROM YOUR MISTAKES
The questing mind looks for the reasons for mistakes and builds up a body
of experience that helps it to make good decisions in the future.

⟫ EXTEND YOUR HORIZONS
You can do this by reading, travelling, listening to the radio or to TED talks,
watching TV or taking an interest in the arts, sciences and politics.

⟫ BE ABLE TO ARGUE A POINT – WITH AN OPEN MIND
The questing mind takes issue with others' opinions from time to time but
is open to persuasion. Learning can take place during disagreement.

⟫ MAKE AN EFFORT TO SAY WHAT YOU MEAN
This often requires thinking before you speak. Empathy is helpful, as it enables
you to hear what you are saying from another's point of view. That way, it's easier
to judge whether you have conveyed your meaning accurately.

⟫ AVOID PARROTING RECEIVED OPINIONS
You may agree with the majority opinion, but this should happen because you
have weighed the evidence and come to a conclusion. You should not hesitate
to express a minority view when it's something you truly believe in.

Making relationships
WORK

When relationships present challenges, it's worth asking yourself whether you are at least partly responsible. The best relationships tend to be those we consciously nurture, applying empathy, compassion and generosity to strengthen the bond, and communicating well for mutual understanding.

We are, in a sense, islands – despite the poet John Donne's avowal that "No man is an island" – but we send signals out to other islands and receive signals back. In this way, contact, friendship and community are formed. Often the two-way traffic of signals becomes charged with the ultimate value: love. Rewarding relationships don't usually happen automatically. Sometimes, at the beginning, you may indeed feel that a relationship is self-seeding, growing without any apparent effort from either party. This is true of both romantic relationships and friendships. However, even such bonds may reach a point where a little corrective gardening is needed. To continue the metaphor, a relationship will often benefit from:

➲ NURTURE
The seeds may have rooted, but growth may fail unless you take positive steps to communicate well, be patient and compassionate with each other, and be sensitive to each other's needs. Each party should also make it clear to the other what the possibilities for the relationship seem to be, from their perspective.

➲ WEEDING
This refers to tackling any issues that arise. All sorts of misunderstandings, resentments and irritations may take root, and tension may be caused when people have contrasting sets of priorities. Compromise and good, empathic communication are good weeding tools.

➲ SEEDING
Find new ways to communicate. If something has not worked in the past, trying the same thing with more force is unlikely to help. Instead, do something new and stop focusing on the problem. Consider new ideas about what you would like to do together.

"They whose minds are filled with kindness will never enter a world dark with woes."
TIRUVALLUVAR (c.1st century BCE)

The relationship
PENTANGLE

Below is a five-point programme for enriching any relationship. Follow it to make your connections with others more honest, more giving and more easeful.

1 EMPATHIZE

Empathy is our intuitive understanding of others, which makes us sympathize and appreciate, with warm feelings. When the relationship is not strong enough to encourage deep empathy (for example, your contact with a financial adviser you see once a year), there's a less intimate form of appreciation that we tend to call "respect".

2 SHOW KINDNESS

The open heart is not only compassionate; it also looks for ways to show this. "Kindness" is a catch-all term appropriate to every level of contact. Thinking about the needs of others and how to help to satisfy them gives us the peaceful sense of deep, loving purpose.

5 STEP BACK FROM CONFLICT

When a disagreement starts turning heated, make a conscious effort to observe your own emotions and form a positive intention to be responsive rather than reactive. See if you can reach out and mend the fracture. Avoid getting stuck in your sense of being in the right.

3 COMMUNICATE

Barriers are often broken down by open, flexible communication. This means avoiding platitudes and empty soundbites and conveying your meaning with sincerity, tact and warmth. Body language is also important – especially hugging and touching, when appropriate.

4 FORGIVE

When you sense resentment building, ask yourself what is stopping you from forgiving. Give people the opportunity to show the best of themselves now and in the future, rather than dwelling on past hurts. Always let them come back into your life in a refreshed relationship.

Home is where
THE HEART IS

For many, the home is a place of refuge and love. When things go wrong there, the stress is doubly felt. Resolve home issues through mutual support, through patience or compromise, or, in the case of household emergencies, through a willingness to invest money without being unduly anxious.

"Home" is a word charged with emotion. Its connotations include relief at being in a safe space, surrounded by love and by beloved things, such as furniture, fabrics, photographs and heirlooms. It's the locus of our emotional being, the clinic where stresses come to be healed – often from a day at work.

Personalizing the home exerts a measure of control over our environment. This, in itself, is satisfying, as is the opportunity for self-expression. Homemaking is creative, and those who believe they have no such talents may in fact be exercising creativity in their home setting. To see the home as a canvas for self-expression is to release a vital psychological benefit.

Sharing

A home you share is a cooperative enterprise, with opportunities for affirming the bond of love or friendship through joint decision-making. The ego is placed on hold, as amicable agreement is reached on personal, shared and communal spaces or on the division of routine labour.

The Austrian poet Rainer Maria Rilke wrote: "I hold this to be the highest task for a bond between two people: that each protects the solitude of the other." The interdependence of a successful relationship is never constrictive: a portion of independence is donated as an aspect of acceptance.

"I had rather be on my farm than be emperor of the world."

GEORGE WASHINGTON (1732–1799)

> "Don't undervalue the near
> while aiming at the far."
>
> EURIPIDES (c.480–c.406 BCE)

Dealing with peace thieves

Of course, problems can manifest around the home, too, undermining its value as a source of heartfelt belonging. Some of the most common issues are given here, with a signpost on how you might choose to deal with them:

➔ RESOLVING RELATIONSHIP TENSIONS

Tackle relationship tensions in specially arranged dialogues outside the home – in a restaurant or café. Your living room or bedroom will not then be linked with open disagreement. And you have the chance of coming back home and making a fresh start.

➔ ACCEPTING INBUILT IMPERFECTIONS

A home that's too small, in the wrong area or lacking a suitable arrangement of rooms can start to cause stress. When the home itself is the problem, rather than a refuge from problems, something can feel fundamentally amiss – like a law enforcement officer committing a crime. The best solution may be to try to restrict thinking or talking about the issue to specific times. Your home still has its many values, despite imperfections, to which you will respond appropriately when you can. These things take time.

➔ DEALING WITH DISRUPTION

A noisy neighbour or unruly child, or builders in the home, can be unsettling. Take whatever practical steps you can to minimize the impact, meanwhile taking comfort from the fact that the situation is temporary. With the neighbour, try having them round for a social occasion, where you can gently put across your point of view.

➔ TACKLING DYSFUNCTION

A problem with the plumbing, electricity or drains, or a flood in the home, can cause disruption, demand your time and cost money to fix. Draw upon your resilience (see pages 69–71), resist the temptation to turn it into a catastrophe, and take comfort and practical help from loved ones and friends. Having to spend money often feels painful more on a matter of principle than in the way it truly affects your quality of life.

Finding your
BLESSINGS

3 AFFIRMATIONS

→ "I have wonderful friends and family around me. I'm offering thanks to them continually, through my loving interactions and thoughts."

→ "I'm blessed to be myself, for within myself I'm finding ways to make the best possible use of all the opportunities that surround me."

→ "I'm walking a path rich in positive experiences and valuable lessons. Whatever surprises me, enriches me."

7 THOUGHT POINTS

→ Review your self-awareness

Assess yourself in terms of these six factors: motivations, preferences, personality, assumptions, reactions and needs. For each factor, just write down single words that come as close as you can get to capturing how you are. Under "personality", write a few adjectives; under "reactions", write what tends to trigger emotions in you. Then consider how these different elements affect your judgment, decisions and interactions. Self-reflection of this kind can yield valuable insights. Devoting half an hour or more specifically to the analysis tends to be more productive than allowing your mind to wander at random over these issues.

→ Value loving kindness

Treating loving kindness as your true north will bring you contentment at a deep level. Ask yourself how widely you can spread warmth and compassion in your life. Could you let go of your ego enough to show loving kindness, not just to your inner circle of partner, family and friends, but to acquaintances or even old enemies? Familiarize yourself with the loving kindness meditation known as *metta*, which involves sending loving feelings to a series of people in turn (see page 137). Bear in mind that the starting point is *self*-compassion – acceptance of yourself with all your quirks and imperfections.

➔ Feel joy for others

Think of the people who mean most to you and start by meditating or reflecting on how grateful you are for what they give you. Then morph to embracing their positive qualities and achievements as warmly and joyfully as if they were your own. Feel selfless pride in their contribution to their world. Then move seamlessly from pride back to gratitude. Use this exercise whenever you detect any tendency in yourself towards dissatisfaction with whatever life is bringing your way.

➔ Cultivate 360-degree vision

Curiosity is a sign of real engagement with life – seeking to know more about the people you meet, the people you know already, the artefacts and nature that surround you, the ideas and opinions you come across. Take this further by showing curiosity way beyond the limits of your known horizons. Think about your nation, other nations, the world, the solar system and how it fits into the cosmos as a whole. Let your exploration be shaped by what fascinates you and by what you see, hear and read about.

➔ Pursue paradoxes

Life's deepest truths are often paradoxical. The end of our travelling will be to arrive at our starting point and know the place for the first time, as the poet T.S. Eliot believed. You may find happiness in the course of seeking something else entirely. Or, to quote a Zen saying, "You cannot tread the path before you become the path itself." Relish paradox wherever you find it. You might look specifically at the Zen *koans* (paradoxical questions used in meditation). Also, bear in mind that life's richest insights often defy rational explanation and even involve an element of contradiction.

➔ Celebrate the ordinary

The near-at-hand is often neglected, as people look for rewarding experiences outside their immediate context. If you are interested in other people's lives, have a chat to the woman you see every day outside the superstore holding a charity collecting box. If you love nature, watch the robin in your garden making its dummy nests to fool predators. Often you will find greatness in ordinary people – for example, in their heroism in the face of adversity. Delve near and be inspired.

➔ Put age in perspective

Value people for themselves, whatever their age. Some of the most rewarding friendships are intergenerational. Steer clear of society's ageist stereotypes: the young as shallow, unformed; the elderly as conservative, obsolescent. Look for wisdom in children. If you talk to kids, you will certainly find it, often in the form of refreshingly unprejudiced insights. Be alert, too, for nimble thinking, openness and positivity in those who have more decades of life experience than you.

ACTION PLAN

Enjoying the FRUITS

10 ACTION POINTS

➔ Write your manifesto

Contentment does not mean complacency: embracing change in carefully selected areas in a positive spirit is part of the richness of our experience. Try, as a self-awareness exercise, writing your personal manifesto. If you are unclear about your goals, this process will help you frame them; it will also enable you to know what parts of your life are working just as you would like.

➔ Give habitually

Seneca, the Roman philosopher, put it well: "We should give as we would receive, cheerfully, quickly and without hesitation; for there is no grace in a benefit that sticks to the fingers." Remember, though, that if you are too conscious of being generous, you are in danger of shading into self-congratulation. The most valuable gift is some portion of yourself. Getting into the habit of giving fills you with karmic credit that will help you feel at ease with yourself.

➔ Join in celebration

Grasp every opportunity to take part in celebration – birthday or anniversary parties, street parties, carnivals, festivals. Collective celebration generates a positive ambience that can be relaxing and uplifting. Relish the crossing point of many different pathways. Whenever you can, take opportunities to contribute to the speechmaking. On your own birthday, why not surprise people by handing out little gifts?

➔ Contribute to group enjoyment

Find a group of people pursuing together an interest or hobby that attracts you. It might be a book group, a walking club, a knitting circle or an archery society. There's usually a fascinating dynamic of personalities, with opportunities to learn about lives that are different from your own. Also to be valued is the mindful engagement with a particular focus. Combining mindfulness with sociability is conducive to well-being.

◯ Consciously connect

In your intimate relationships, be sure not only to touch and hug but also to really look. Familiarity can make our eyes glaze over, but true connection lies in truly looking, even at a face you have lived with for ages. You should be able to notice small signs of stress or tiredness, and therefore be prompted to offer sympathy and support.

◯ Talk and listen mindfully

Talking is a form of fitness regime for our powers of self-expression. By talking nimbly and articulately, we send out signals. The clearer these signals are, the more valuable will be the responses we receive. While the other person is responding, we need to switch to listening mode – not planning what we are going to say next. A good conversation requires thoughtful input and output. Paying close attention to both sides of an exchange, in the moment, brings immense rewards.

◯ Respect the body

Your body, whatever the shape or size, is a gift you would do well not to squander. Look after your physical health and fitness as you would someone else's welfare you had promised to safeguard – an assurance that you are taking your purpose seriously. Rejoice in health and fitness if you are fortunate enough to have them.

◯ Follow truth

There are several dimensions to truthfulness, just as there are several dimensions to love. One is your truth to yourself – the value to be found in authenticity. To be authentic is to have a good measure of self-awareness, with the minimum of self-delusion, and to project your real self to others as much as you can. Another is being honest with other people, even when it's easier or more convenient for you to lie or mislead; however, avoiding unnecessary hurt by blunt speaking is itself a kind of truth – reflecting the importance of compassion.

◯ Commit to work

Many of us who work do so only to make a living. If we won the lottery, we would no doubt find other things to do with our time. However, even if work holds no intrinsic interest for you in principle, in practice you can draw meaning and value from it by committing yourself wholeheartedly to doing the best job you can. The alternative is to let work fill your time. Instead, let your energy and skills fill work's particular purposes, while giving you the opportunity to learn and grow.

◯ Keep the brain active

For as long as your brain is active, stretch it on a regular basis, in the mental equivalent of physical training. Read challenging books or articles, engage with ideas, do brain puzzles or debate controversial topics with friends. Like a spade in the garden, your brain will shine brighter with use.

How to find
DEEP PEACE

True inner peace is a weave of the self within the mind and heart. It rests in large part on the foundation of love, the ultimate human value. However, love within a couple can go astray, and it's common for partners to take each other for granted and for tensions to grow over time. By attending closely to the quality of a partnership, keeping communication open and honest, and investing real effort to keep the bond glowing with vitality, we can grow love as an enriching environment for everyday life and a basis for being giving and compassionate to humankind as a whole.

CHAPTER 6

"The soul unfolds itself, like a
lotus of countless petals."

KAHLIL GIBRAN (1883–1931)

Alongside love, the other cornerstone of deep peace
is spirit – or, rather, the harmonization of body, mind
and spirit that puts us in alignment with our own
being and with life as a whole. Through reflection on
spiritual concepts and regular practice of a discipline
such as meditation or yoga, we can take ourselves to
a new level of awareness and peace.

Nurturing
LOVE

Love can be fierce and needy or relaxed and refreshing. Here are some thoughts about how love can develop into the most mature and supportive of connections, each safeguarding the inner peace of the other through empathy, compassion and support.

Our loving relationships are often threaded together with ties of emotional need. This is the basis of jealousy. It also explains why couples often stay together even after they have identified fundamental incompatibilities in the way they each choose to live. If we can progress our self-valuing in a way that makes us emotionally stronger, we can move away from dependency and adopt a more open-hearted, more giving attitude. This moves us into a truer and more perceptive relationship with our loved ones.

Although the highest love flows in all directions from an open heart, many of us seek an intimate bond with one person, founded on close togetherness, sex, probably having children and certainly romantic love, which may become less romantic but deeper as the years pass. Such love gathers strength over time and with the mutual experience of life's ups and downs, one person giving encouragement and support to the other. After years of being together, a telepathy may develop, each partner able to guess what the other is thinking and feeling.

Shared destiny
Ideally, the initial romantic impulse matures into something more profound, involving body, heart and mind – and also spirit. We commit to another person, who remains an independent agent yet participates with us in a shared destiny that seems second nature to both. When paths do diverge, as often happens, this doesn't have to be a disaster if each shows the other gratitude for time spent together and compassion in the current situation.

The two-way traffic of openness and empathy in a successful relationship enlarges the possibilities of happiness for both. If there are tensions, this four-step strategy is a good way to tackle them:

1 Enter a place of peace together and silently just be, putting your issues on hold. Hold hands and mindfully appreciate your togetherness.
2 Agree on a time and place (ideally outside the home) for a constructive talk – leave at least a few hours after your silent togetherness.
3 At the chosen time and place, engage in open, compassionate communication. In the event of any negative emotions arising, either party is entitled to say "Empathy break" and start the process anew.

An eye-gazing
MEDITATION

This meditation for any two people who have a close bond, or maybe are developing one, encourages an attentive connection. It recognizes otherness, while reaching out warmly and trustingly in love.

➡ Sit opposite each other in two kitchen-type chairs, faces only about a metre apart.

➡ Look at (not into) each other's eyes, as objectively as you can. Do this until you find yourself inspecting the eye and its surroundings mindfully, without any sense of personality. Pay particular attention to the pupils and irises. Spend about five minutes on this.

➡ At a nod from partner A, switch to a different mode of looking. This time, look into the pupils, as if into a dark room, and imagine your partner's spirit there – the full energy of their being. Reach out to that spirit with love and compassion. Again, do this for about five minutes.

➡ At a nod from partner B, switch back to objective looking. Give silent thanks for the body, mind and spirit – the entirety – of your partner. Conclude by saying "I love you", feeling the truth of the words with all your heart.

4 Find places where you can agree on a way forwards. Stop any habits that create uncomfortable feelings in your relationship and commit instead to doing new things that reinforce positive feelings.

We should not necessarily expect love to be easy – growth seldom is. But if we work at fine-tuning our loving bond with a partner with awareness, compassion and gratitude in a spirit of mutual exploration and support, we may well be fortunate enough to tune in to one of the most rewarding experiences possible. And then, secure in our mutual love, we can happily extend the meaning of connection through showing a less intimate kind of love to others.

"Love is the only sane and satisfactory answer to the problem of human existence."

ERICH FROMM (1900–1980)

Journey
OF THE SPIRIT

The spirit's existence, though outside the scope of science, is deeply felt by people of many different faiths. As we journey through life, we grow in spiritual awareness. It's the spirit that gives us our deepest sense of kinship with humankind as a whole.

We often hear about the importance of nourishing the spirit. A better way to put this is that the spirit nourishes all other branches of our lives. Our deepest happiness is best served not by working on the spirit to develop it in any way, but by ceasing to do those things in our lives that inhibit its full flowering – such as withholding love because we ration it to a handful of people we like.

The network of kinship

Most people who believe in spirit see it as connecting all humanity. It's the thing that instils the life of every individual with more than biological or moral meaning, while informing a global network of kinship – like blood circulating through a body. Empathy and compassion happen when we tune into this system, feeling a common bond with those who share our network.

If we pursue this analogy of the bloodstream, and ask what is the equivalent of the pumping heart, the answer will vary. Some people will say "God" or "the One" or "the Divine". Others find no need to name the source of all energy but are content to bask in its radiance. Others again engage in a lifelong spiritual quest, sometimes swinging between faith and doubt.

Mystery and awareness

We live inside and among the inexhaustible mystery of the human being. Outside our skins but inside our minds are natural beauty, ingenious nature, the awe-inspiring night sky and the astonishing products of human creativity. In sharp contrast to that is the devastation we have brought, through war and environmental damage.

There are, of course, additional complications: death, sickness, chance and "evil". Suffering will impact on our lives at some point. But if we are compassionate, we will see those others who are suffering and will reach out to them with love and, if we can, with practical support of some kind.

The journey of spirit will take us through places of darkness as well as light. We can find a way of peace if we believe in ourselves and our core values, pursue true awareness, live in the moment, accept what we cannot change, give and receive love, rejoice in life's amazing gifts, and cultivate and honour our best intentions.

WONDER WALL

Imagine you are in a cosmic museum, looking at the prize exhibit in the foyer: a mosaic of life's most wonderful and mysterious aspects. All these cosmic highlights are reasons to give thanks, and also to undertake a personal exploration in a questing frame of mind. Ponder the imponderables itemized below. Resolve to reflect on them all further as you continue your life's journey.

- >> The mystery of human existence – or just existence
- >> The enigma of cosmic origins
- >> The phenomenal sophistication of human biology – or just biology
- >> The unfathomable relationship between mind and matter
- >> The magnificence and immensity of the unknowable cosmos
- >> The beauty of nature and the beauty created by humankind
- >> The sublime contribution made to humankind by loving, compassionate, self-sacrificing and courageous souls

"It would be idle to say that life is a steady progression in happiness. But it is most certain that in the natural course of things a healthy soul grows continually richer until its latest day on earth."

GEORGE S. MERRIAM (1843–1914)

Lessons from
THE EAST

The East has long been the source of profound ideas about the nature of existence and ways to generate peace. Buddhism, in particular, has contributed powerful concepts and inspiring exemplars – not least the Buddha himself, who taught the importance of letting go of our attachments.

Every morning, in Chinese public parks, clusters of people take part in Tai Chi, an ancient practice with slow, balletic movements, originally evolved for self-defence and repurposed for inner peace. Many practitioners are likely to be elderly. If a regular attendant fails to turn up one day, someone goes to their home to check on their well-being. Contrast this communal aspect with isolated, music-fuelled workouts at the gym.

It's easy to become entranced by a romanticized vision of the East – the charm of haiku, the paradoxes of Zen, the scholar hermit in his hut. However, once we penetrate the clichés, we find wisdom that is relevant to our lives in the West today – and to our search for inner peace.

The Buddhist way

Much of what we take from the East comes from Buddhism. The Buddha taught a way to deal with suffering that involves letting go of attachment – to pleasure, desire, comfort, the past. All will fade; hence the suffering. By mindful attention to ourselves, through meditation, we can cease to crave. Mindfulness practice today draws from Buddhism the idea that, by inhabiting the moment, we can build tranquillity and insight and foster love and compassion.

The 14th Dalai Lama, most famous of contemporary Buddhists, radiates easeful, companionable goodness and humour. Yet he is actively engaged in humanity's suffering, working to bring about a more compassionate world, interracial harmony and the preservation of Tibet's culture and natural beauty. He ends a Facebook post with a simple plea that shows there's nothing complex or detached about true spirituality:

"In short, may I request you please to help others whenever you can and if for some reason you can't do that, at least to refrain from doing anyone any harm."

HIS HOLINESS THE 14TH DALAI LAMA

ORIENTATION POINTS

Here are some of the ideas derived from Eastern thinking that can offer useful signposts in our pursuit of the way of peace. Spend some time contemplating the relevance of these notions to your own experience. Explore further, online or in the many books on these subjects.

IMPERMANENCE

Buddhism asserts that all conditioned existence, without exception, is "transient, evanescent, inconstant". Our ego mind will tell us we will live forever, but mortal life is finite. Our mind may tell us that our difficulties are permanent but, similarly, they are not. Meditating on this idea helps us to treat each moment as precious.

KARMA

This is the Buddhist law of appropriate consequences. Although originally related to the idea of a person's behaviour determining their level of being in the next life, these days "karma" is a useful term for the moral credit we obtain by acting virtuously. Central to it is the image of every action's effects rippling out far-reachingly into the world.

MANTRA

Used in meditation, particularly in Tantric Buddhism, a mantra is a set of powerful words or sounds. The Western equivalent is the affirmation, by which we assert a positive belief about ourselves. The energy of that affirmation makes it self-fulfilling.

NIRVANA

Those who attain Nirvana, the state of perfect enlightenment realized through meditation, no longer accumulate karmic consequences and will no longer be reborn into *samsara* – the cycle of constant rebirth in which all beings are trapped. "Enlightenment" is usually an exaggerated word used by the modern-day seeker who draws upon Buddhist wisdom without committing to a radically spiritual lifestyle.

AWARENESS

The experience of awareness is expressed economically in "Be here now", which comes from a 1971 book of the same name on yogic spirituality, written by Ram Dass (born Richard Alpert), who was quoting the guru with whom he travelled in India. The power of the phrase comes from its intersection of living (being) with two dimensions: place and time. This is the essence of mindfulness.

TAO

Chinese thinking features the concept of living intuitively in the spirit of the Tao, which means "path" or "way", a mystic natural order that informs the whole universe. The *Tao Te Ching*, an ancient Chinese text sacred to the religion of Taoism, emphasizes counter-rational truths – for example, how weakness can overcome strength.

Following a
PRACTICE

Anyone interested in finding deep peace, rather than merely a way to be more relaxed, is going to want to explore one or more formal practices – perhaps meditating every day, with a weekly session in one of the body disciplines, such as Tai Chi or Qi Gong. Some options and pointers are offered here.

Cherry-picking from different religions to create your own personalized faith is often criticized as inauthentic. However, in the mind–body–spirit realm a mixed approach is to be encouraged – for example, daily meditation combined with weekly yoga, Tai Chi or Pilates. All the mainstream disciplines have universal benefits and will serve you well, alone or in combination. Some of the practices that exist more towards the fringe may also be worth exploring – it's up to the individual to choose what works for them.

Spaces for growth

Yoga, meditation, prayer and mindfulness practice all provide a space for the spirit as well as the mind and body. They enhance our health and well-being (this is increasingly confirmed by scientific research), promote our personal growth and can also help to deepen our connections with others. When we are quiet and still, we can find the best part of ourselves, discarding what does not serve us and choosing what does. Meditation and other practices take quiet and stillness (or gentle movement) to a new dimension, allowing us to pick up subtle signals that can guide our lives more truthfully. They enable us to step outside our everyday anxieties and be who we really are.

Given that the choice of disciplines is wide and that different people are drawn to different ones, here are some general guidelines that may help as you experiment to find the chemistry that suits you.

- ⊘ **TAKE A CLASS** If you can afford it, taking a regular class is great. The sense of kinship among a well-taught group is an important extra benefit. A class is especially useful for any kind of physical work – it's easy to get things wrong on your own.
- ⊘ **WATCH AND LISTEN** Before committing to a class, ask if you can attend as an observer. Or, at least, meet and chat to the teacher or leader, and make a judgment based on your intuition.
- ⊘ **BE PATIENT** Don't be in a rush to decide whether the class, once started, is working for you. So long as it feels right, keep going. The benefits can be deep and not easily detectable on the surface.

A meditation ROAD MAP

The beauty of meditation is that you can do it virtually anywhere. This makes it an excellent practice to do daily or every few days, alongside a weekly class. It means you can still have a practice in your life while on holiday or on a business trip.

 OBJECT MEDITATION

The idea is to develop focus and learn how to avoid mental distraction. The focus may be a mandala (sacred diagram) or something like a candle flame.

 MANTRA MEDITATION

Reciting a mantra (such as "om"), you release accumulated stresses. Mantras may be chanted or spoken softly.

 **KUNDALINI MEDITATION**

This is a deep yoga meditation to awaken kundalini energy (at the base of the spine) and bring about deep enlightenment.

 **MINDFULNESS MEDITATION**

Many people do this versatile practice in eight-week courses – as mindfulness-based stress reduction (MBSR). You focus on sensations in the moment, without judging yourself.

 INSIGHT MEDITATION

This is also known as Vipassana ("seeing things as they really are") meditation. You attend to your breathing, while noticing thoughts or emotions.

 METTA BHAVANA

This is "loving kindness meditation". First, you send loving kindness to the self, then loved ones, then people you feel neutral about, and then people you find challenging.

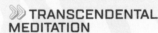 **TRANSCENDENTAL MEDITATION**

A form of mantra meditation, with a specific mantra given to each student. This meditation is highly structured and institutionalized.

As well as the body disciplines, there are practices such as cognitive behaviour therapy (CBT) and neuro-linguistic programming (NLP) aimed at changing our responses. In addition, there are one-to-one therapy sessions, the most popular of which is counselling. This may be helpful in a range of situations, and not just when you are in crisis.

Exploring the
WHOLE SELF

3 AFFIRMATIONS

➡ "I'm not my body, or my mind. I'm a holistic being infused with spirit.
I'm infinitely precious and infinitely capable of growth."

➡ "I'm delving down through layers of awareness towards the deep peace
that lies at the heart of the cosmos."

➡ "I'm spreading love in all directions from the infinite supply bestowed upon
us all by the Divine."

7 THOUGHT POINTS

➡ Be committed

Whatever kind of intimate relationship you are in, be committed to it in the same
way that you are committed to your values. If fractures appear, don't use them as
the excuse for breaking that commitment. Treat the bond between two souls as a
holistic phenomenon involving the spirit. If you are unmarried, devise a ceremony
to affirm your love in public. Renew your vows from time to time. Retain an
independent spirit within a framework of unshakable love.

➡ Think big thoughts

Don't be daunted by the large questions of life – matters concerning God, spirit
and destiny. Dip into theology and philosophy, and consider doing a formal
course in some aspect or another. Philosophers start with basic questions, and
none of these is unavailable to you as an amateur. Treat your own conclusions
seriously – your view matters, in the context of who you are.

➡ Engage with ritual

Every religion is a complex tradition, combining history, myth, ritual and belief.
All these strands are thought-provoking. Consider such questions as "Are miracles
symbolic or literal?"; "What is the value of ritual?"; "What kind of hero was Jesus?"

Attend services now and then. Even if formal religion has no part in your life, open yourself to its insights.

➲ Affirm the spirit

Contemplate the spirit and consider the role it has in your life. Is it the same as the soul, or does it imply a more universal life force that transcends the individual? Whatever your faith, read agnostic/atheist texts such as the works of Richard Dawkins and Christopher Hitchens and see if you can find holes in their arguments. Their target is religion, but perhaps they are taking sideswipes at spirit, too? If so, how would you defend it?

➲ Explore Buddhism

The truths of Buddhism are uncomfortable but life-affirming. Study the Buddha's life and read the *Dhammapada*, one of the most popular Buddhist scriptures. Familiarize yourself with the Four Noble Truths and the Noble Eightfold Path (perfect understanding, perfect thought, perfect speech, perfect action, perfect livelihood, perfect effort, perfect mindfulness and perfect concentration). Explore Zen Buddhism, too, with its deceptively simple philosophy of encountering life directly, without the mediation of language or logic. Meditate on impermanence.

➲ Harmonize with nature

This is the message of the *Tao Te Ching*, complied in the 6th to 4th centuries BCE. A key concept is *wu wei*, which means "non-doing" – in the sense of not doing anything counter to the flow of nature. *Wu wei* is a wakeful ease that allows us – even without effort – to respond to situations as they happen. It's related to the Buddhist idea of nonattachment to the ego. Read the *Tao Te Ching* and relish its poetry: "We pierce doors and windows to make a house. And it is in these spaces where there is nothing that the house is useful to us."

➲ Tap into energy

The Chinese word *qi* (or *chi*) and the Indian term *prana* refer to the life force – a universal energy within our bodies that cannot be measured by science. When you focus your mind on a part of the body, you are displacing energy there – as the Chinese say, "*Chi* follows *yi*" (*yi* is intention/attention). This energy is the basis of acupuncture, reiki, the chakras and the yogic *mudras* (hand gestures). Explore *qi* and *prana* in your reading, and think about what energy means for you. You can learn to detect it between the palms of your hands when you hold them facing each other.

ACTION PLAN

Going deeper into PEACE

10 ACTION POINTS

➔ Be authentic

Divesting yourself of any pretension or self-importance is often the key to stripping away social anxiety and the sense that life has disadvantaged you. The authentic self has no truck with such assessments. It's the learning, growing self, aware of its potential and making the choices most likely to lead to the realization of that potential. To be authentic to yourself means being open-hearted with others. Truth and love, a powerful combination, flow from authenticity.

➔ Simplify

Do the 10–10–10 challenge from time to time. That is, think of 10 items to recycle or dispose of, 10 to donate and 10 to go back to where they belong. This is a fun spin on the serious benefits of decluttering. Start with the home, move on to your work space and your computer, and then progress to aspects of your life as a whole. Simplifying enhances the free flow of the spirit.

➔ Take mindfulness further

Mindfulness is intentionally bringing awareness either to physical sensations or to thoughts or feelings, without judging yourself. If your attention wanders, you observe this forgivingly, then return your focus to the matter in hand. Do something mindfully every day – whether being fully attentive to a chore (such as washing the car) or engaging in a mindfulness meditation on the sensations you feel within your body. Mindfulness gives you insight into your emotions, reduces brain chatter, helps you to connect, lowers stress and improves concentration.

➔ Do Tai Chi or yoga

Consider doing Tai Chi or yoga on a regular basis. Tai Chi was originally a martial art but is now a healing therapy; yoga is a lifestyle practice with a spiritual dimension. Both practices seek an integration of the self. A simplified distinction might be: in Tai Chi, you relax to stretch; in yoga, you stretch to relax. For a more Western low-impact exercise, try Pilates, which focuses on balance, posture, strength and flexibility.

➔ Visit spiritual places

An encounter with a building or landscape that is in some way spiritual can be refreshing at the deepest level of being. Places of worship qualify, but the most evocative spots are temples, chapels or monasteries set in a wilderness, where natural magnificence joins forces with the power of faith. Ruined temples and churches can have a natural beauty, especially when nature reclaims them.

➔ Just sit and look

Go to a viewpoint that looks out onto an attractive landscape or cityscape. Just sit quietly (on a bench, if there is one), empty your mind of thoughts and emotions, admire the view … and see what happens. You may find yourself meditating without even knowing it. But don't even think about whether you are or not. Just look and be grateful for what you see.

➔ Share new experiences

With your partner or family, or a friend, break out into new territory – literally and metaphorically. This is a great way to affirm and protect the strength of relationships, through an injection of variety and joy. Undertake a course together, and encourage each other as you learn. Make an ambitious travel plan – even if you cannot afford it till next year or the year after. Break out of your comfort zones in different ways, and relish the spirit of shared adventure.

➔ Spread love

Experiencing love for humankind as a whole, and for people you meet but don't know, is one of the most reliable foundations for a happy life. The starting point is self-compassion. Once you show love to yourself, you will find yourself with an abundance of loving energy. Direct it to others in meditation (see page 137) and in charitable generosity. Let love spill everywhere. Make it your default position, preventing resentment, envy and other negative emotions from ever seeding.

➔ Undertake a pilgrimage

Some places are special for their association with a special person – maybe a saint, an artist or writer, or a selfless campaigner. Honour the contribution made by one of your heroes by devising a pilgrimage to sites where they made a difference. For example, if you are an animal lover, you might visit Assisi, home of St Francis. Or go on one of the great religious pilgrimage routes, such as the road to Santiago della Compostela, in Spain. Experience a journey of the spirit.

➔ Offer service

One of the keys to happiness is to be of service to others. Make this a priority in your personal manifesto. Use your intuition to discern what people's needs are, then compassionately help them to meet those needs. As Mother Teresa said, "Do not wait for leaders: do it alone, person to person."

INDEX

Mike Annesley is the author of DK's **PRACTICAL MINDFULNESS** and a published poet with six volumes of poetry to his credit, including a long prose poem based on the I Ching. His poetic imagination, and his deep absorption in the Mind Body Spirit ethos, have shaped (behind the scenes) dozens of successful illustrated MBS titles for the international market.

Steve Nobel is an author, book mentor and spiritual coach, and was the director of Alternatives for 13 years – a leading UK group running weekly Mind Body Spirit events dedicated to raising spiritual awareness. He is also the founder of Soul Matrix Healing, designed to open the gateway to our soul's potential.

picture credits

The Noun Project (thenounproject.com)

acknowledgements

Eddison Books Limited
Creative Consultant **Nick Eddison**
Managing Editor **Tessa Monina**
Editor **John Andrews**
Design **Jane McKenna** (www.fogdog.co.uk)
Indexer **Marie Lorimer**
Production **Sarah Rooney & Cara Clapham**